OSCAR NIEMEYER and the Architecture of Brazil

OSCAR NIEMEYER and the Architecture of Brazil

David Underwood

For Liliana, Leigh, and Melissa, and Joel and Helen

First published in the United States of America
in 1994 by Rizzoli International Publications, Inc.
300 Park Avenue South, New York, New York 10010

Copyright © 1994 Rizzoli International Publications, Inc.

Library of Congress Cataloging-in-Publication Data
Underwood, David Kendrick.
Oscar Niemeyer and the architecture of Brazil /
David Underwood.
p.   cm.
Includes bibliographical references.
ISBN 0-8478-1686-9 (HC). —
ISBN 0-8478-1687-7 (PB).
1. Niemeyer, Oscar, 1907– —Criticism and inter-
pretation. 2. International style (Architecture)—Brazil.
I. Title.
NA859.N5U54 1994   94-11866
720'.92—dc20   CIP

Front cover illustration: Oscar Niemeyer, Planalto
Palace, Brasília, 1957–58. Photograph by Toni
Cumella and Ramon Sirvent, courtesy of Josep Mª
Botey, *Oscar Niemeyer*
Back cover illustration: Oscar Niemeyer, Maison de
la Culture, Le Havre, 1972–82. Photograph by Toni
Cumella and Ramon Sirvent, courtesy of Josep Mª
Botey, *Oscar Niemeyer*
Pages 2–3: Rio de Janeiro from Sugar Loaf Mountain,
showing Copacabana Beach (left) and Corcovado
Mountain (far right). Photograph by David
Underwood
Pages 6–7: Rio de Janeiro, with Sugar Loaf Mountain
and Botafogo Bay. Photograph by David Underwood

Designed by Lawrence Wolfson,
Printed in Hong Kong

Contents

Preface

Brazilian architect Oscar Niemeyer Soares Filho's seminal contribution to the history of modern architecture is unquestioned, yet a deeper understanding of his work has long been needed. Practicing for more than half a century, Niemeyer has become one of the world's most prolific, persistent, and polemical innovators of modernism—and one of the few remaining champions of the heroic values that gave birth to this movement. As the eighty-six-year-old architect continues to turn out projects from his studio overlooking Copacabana Beach in Rio de Janeiro, this monograph remains necessarily incomplete.

Given Niemeyer's long career and his stature in the history of modernism, the paucity of solid critical and historical literature on him seems strange. Appreciation of his contributions has no doubt been hindered by a cultural ethnocentrism prevalent in Europe and North America that tends to dismiss Latin American achievements as derivative, peripheral, and generally inferior. The consensus that utopian modernism was an unmitigated failure, therefore less worthy of art-historical attention than the more "advanced" contributions of postmodernism, has not helped matters. Brasília has received ample attention and criticism, most notably in the work of Norma Evenson and more recently James Holston, but an English-language monograph treating Niemeyer's entire career and its relationship to Brazilian society has long been lacking. This book attempts to fill that gap. While I have benefited from the numerous secondary studies published in various languages, I have attempted to approach the man and his monuments afresh, focusing on formal and contextual analysis and relying on primary source material collected from the archive of the Niemeyer Foundation in Rio. Because Niemeyer's post-Brasília achievements and their relationship to his earlier work are not widely known, I have concentrated on charting the architect's stylistic evolution and explaining the significance of his most important projects within the broader sociopolitical framework of modern Brazil.

I would like to thank first Oscar Niemeyer himself, who gave me access to drawings and documents in the archives of his foundation and received me warmly in his office on numerous occasions between 1990 and the present. The architect also permitted me to reproduce many black-and-white photographs from his office files. Without the assistance of the staff of his office and foundation, among whom I must single out his granddaughter, Ana Lúcia Niemeyer de Medeiros, and his able office administrator, Maria Lourdes de Faro, I could never have completed the research for this book. My work in Brasília was facilitated by Fernando Andrade, who arranged visits to buildings and provided useful information. I have also benefited from interviews with those involved personally with Niemeyer or the modern movement in Brazil, most notably Max Abramovitz, George Dudley, Lúcio Costa, Roberto Burle Marx, and

Antônio Carlos Jobim. I wish to thank as well the five professional photographers of Niemeyer's work, G. E. Kidder-Smith, Paulo Romeo, Michel Moch, John Maier Jr., and Marcel Gautherot, who have generously allowed me to use a number of their superb photographs, and Josep Mª Botey, who allowed us to reproduce photographs from his book *Oscar Niemeyer*.

My research in Brazil was conducted with the support of three travel-research grants awarded by the Rutgers Research Council during the years 1991–93. I also benefited from a semester's leave of absence from the art history department at Rutgers University in New Brunswick. I would like to thank Nicholas Adams, Dennis Dollens, Ronald Christ, and David Brownlee for helpful feedback on an early draft dealing with the Memorial da América Latina in São Paulo. Lisa Vignuolo and Melissa Card Bianco, graduate students in art history at Rutgers, provided efficient and much needed research assistance.

My research in Brazil would not have been possible without the generous collaboration of the Horsa Hotel Chain of Belo Horizonte, Brazil, whose enlightened management provided me with comfortable lodgings in Rio, Brasília, and Belo Horizonte in exchange for this modest acknowledgment. I want to thank as well Francisco, Stella, and Daniel Lisbão for their help and hospitality in São Paulo, and Antônio da Silva of the Brazilian American Cultural Center in New York and Marilene Facciolo of Orlatur in Rio for assistance with travel arrangements and visits in Brazil. I also extend gratitude to Lawrence Wolfson, who designed the book, and to my editors at Rizzoli, David Morton, Elizabeth White, Andrea Monfried, and Lois Nesbitt, for their enthusiasm and interest in the project.

My final and warmest thanks go to my family: to Joel and Helen, for first exposing me to the excitement of foreign cultures and the problems of developing countries; to Lydia, Michael, and Jay; and especially to Liliana, Leigh, and now Melissa, for their love and patient endurance during my long hours of work and trips abroad.

Introduction:
Niemeyer and the Brazilian Dilemma

The architecture of Oscar Niemeyer Soares Filho can be broadly understood as an interaction between two forces: the modernist discourse and the Brazilian milieu. Born on December 15, 1907, in Brazil's old capital, Rio de Janeiro, Niemeyer came of age in a world in transition between the nineteenth and twentieth centuries—between the traditional rural oligarchy of the coffee barons and the modern urban society of the industrial revolution, between a culture of colonial dependency and a new Brazilian society as yet only imagined by modernizing elites increasingly impatient with the European hegemony of beaux-arts eclecticism, best represented in architecture by the grandiose Teatro Municipal (fig. 1), Rio's answer to Charles Garnier's Paris Opéra. The revolt against European academic historicism and the accompanying search for a new cultural identity that was Brazilian and at the same time modern was at the heart of Brazil's modern movement of the 1920s and 1930s. This movement emerged in the wake of two rebel developments: the Modern Art Week held in São Paulo in 1922 and the Regionalist Movement begun in 1926 in Recife and led by sociologist Gilberto Freyre. While the first offered Brazilians an opportunity to explore how avant-garde modernism (especially its fascination with the abstract and the primitive) could become the point of departure for a national alternative to imported styles, the second called attention to unique features of local culture and history that could render modernism truly Brazilian. Missing from these developments was a forceful state patron with the authority, commitment, and resources to translate the new priorities into a nationwide program of social and artistic action.

The circumstances conducive to the synthesis of these developments and their realization on a large scale came with the political revolution of 1930 and the rise of the bureaucratic-authoritarian regime of Getúlio Vargas. The demagogic Vargas regime, in creating the basis for the technocracy, welfare state, and industrial plant of modern Brazil, supplied the vision and energy, the political backing and the public patronage required for the emergence of a new artistic culture that would become synonymous with the nation's technical modernization. As the capital, Rio was naturally the focus of Vargas's ambitious program, which encompassed the creation of several new government ministries and the reform of the outmoded curriculum of the national fine arts academy. Vargas's progressive young minister of education and health, Gustavo Capanema, spearheaded the avant-garde revolution in public architecture by supporting the curricular reforms of Niemeyer's mentor Lúcio Costa, working out the terms of Le Corbusier's epoch-making trip to Brazil in 1936, and overseeing the creation of the first modernist work of monumental public architecture in Latin America: the Ministry of Education and Health Building in Rio. Niemeyer made his debut on

1. Oliveira Passos et al.,
Teatro Municipal, Rio de Janeiro, 1905–9

2. **Oscar Niemeyer** in 1993

3. J. Cardoso Ramalho,
Nossa Senhora da Glória do Outeiro,
Rio de Janeiro, ca. 1730

Rio's architectural scene against the backdrop of the modernizing intentions and Corbusian dispositions of the ministry project.

Niemeyer's negotiation of the Corbusian-Brazilian dialectic was deeply influenced by Costa's mediation. As leader of the modernist camp in the academy whose curriculum he reformed, Costa fostered Brazil's assimilation of modernism by preaching the "scriptures" of what he referred to as "the sacred book of architecture," Le Corbusier's *Vers une architecture* of 1923. The book's compelling combination of five-points specificity and heroic utopian idealism, of the rational and the poetic, of the social and the visual, and of the technical and the formal provided a flexible manifesto that could liberate Brazilian architects from the stale conventions and stifling taboos of the past. Costa initiated the Corbusian project of freeing Brazilians of academic thinking and opened the door to a wider appreciation of Le Corbusier's works and writings. Perhaps most important among the latter were the ten lectures that Le Corbusier delivered in Buenos Aires in 1929, published in Paris a year later as *Précisions*. Outspoken in their lyrical celebration of the exuberant Latin spirit and the dramatic South American landscape, the lectures exemplified Le Corbusier's creative extemporizing and inspired improvisation, a highly personal style that deeply impressed the young Niemeyer.

Costa also championed the baroque architecture of colonial Brazil as an aesthetic model that provided the basis for a nationalistic alternative to European styles. Costa's study of Brazil's earliest buildings fostered in young architects like Niemeyer an appreciation of the structural frankness and formal and volumetric purity of colonial buildings, whose materials and construction techniques were wholly appropriate to the Brazilian environment. Although many of these buildings were really Portuguese, including Niemeyer's favorite, the small church of Nossa Senhora da Glória do Outeiro in Rio (fig. 3), Costa saw the colonial architecture as truer to Brazil than the fashionable facades of the revival and neocolonial styles of the 1920s, which often applied colonial motifs and decoration with little regard to function, material, or underlying structure. Costa's active involvement in the Serviço do Patrimônio Histórico e Artístico Nacional, the new national commission responsible for the preservation of historic monuments, gave him firsthand knowledge of Brazil's colonial heritage. Costa was seriously committed to an art that reflected *Brasilidade*, the authentically Brazilian. Costa's interest in colonial artifacts also enriched his Corbusian view of architecture as above all a plastic art by deepening his appreciation of baroque qualities. Brazilian modernism was profoundly conditioned by renewed interest in the baroque conception of architecture as an expressive sculptural framework for an integrated ensemble characterized by monumental scenography, formal unity, lyrical feeling, and a concern for the transcendental or otherworldly. This conception is clearly visible in the famous Terrace of the Prophets designed by colonial Brazilian sculptor-architect Aleijadinho in Congonhas do Campo (fig. 4) and in his church of São Francisco in Ouro Prêto (fig. 5). Niemeyer's conception of architecture as lyrical sculpture is anchored as much in Costa's appreciation of the colonial baroque as in Le Corbusier's poetic vision. The profound irony is that in trying to escape the cultural imperialism of nineteenth-century Europe and to return to something basic and Brazilian, Brazil's modernists embraced not only another European system but also their own colonial heritage as a defining element of Brazilian identity.

Finally, Costa was important to Niemeyer and the evolution of Brazilian modernism because of his personal humility and idealism: to achieve the best Brazilian architecture possible, Costa repeatedly valued collaborative interaction over personal fame, allowing the talents of men like Niemeyer and landscape architect Roberto Burle Marx to blossom when they might never have surfaced otherwise. On three separate occasions early in Niemeyer's career—the projects for the Ministry of Education and Health Building, the Brazilian Pavilion for the New York World's Fair, and the Grand Hotel in Ouro Preto—Costa stepped aside to let Niemeyer demonstrate and develop his skills. The younger man's fame is thus indebted to what Freyre called the "social plasticity" of his fellow Brazilian. Costa's noble gentility and modest disposition set the tone for the collaborative venture that defined the Brazilian modern movement and led to Niemeyer's best works—many of which would never have been possible without the skillful contributions of structural engineers like Joaquim Cardoso and José Carlos Sussekind, not to mention the thousands of laborers who erected them.

Building on the examples provided by Costa and Le Corbusier, but seeking his own highly personal means of coming to terms with the dialectics of modernism and the Brazilian milieu, Niemeyer has made five major contributions to the history of modern architecture. First, he rapidly assimilated the style and theories of Le Corbusier, personally adapting them to the unique circumstances of his native Brazil. After 1940 Niemeyer quickly advanced beyond the rational architecture of Le Corbusier's five points and the rigid, rectilinear geometry of the International Style to develop a pioneering, free-form modernism that was uniquely Brazilian. Then a period of critical reflection stimulated by the first European criticism of his work and

4. O Aleijadinho (Antônio Francisco Lisboa), **Terrace of the Prophets,** Bom Jesus dos Matosinhos, Congonhas do Campo, Minas Gerais, ca. 1800

5. O Aleijadinho, **São Francisco de Assis,** Ouro Prêto, ca. 1775

his first trip to Europe in 1954 led Niemeyer to develop a bolder yet more disciplined style that culminated in the creation of Brazil's monumental capital city, Brasília. There he daringly reworked classicism to capitalize on the interaction between pure sculptural objects and dramatic physical context—the stark plains and seductive skies of Brazil's vast frontier. The magical and monumental architecture of Brasília was to reflect the ambitious, even surreal project of the city's founders: to lift Brazil out of underdevelopment and advertise the achievement of "fifty years of progress in five."

Niemeyer's quest for a unique utopia based on a modernist monumentality and a heroic redefinition of classicism in modern Brazilian terms was followed by a fourth development: the wider dissemination of his ideas during the period of Brazil's repressive military dictatorship (1964–85), which forced him into exile and led him to elaborate and refine his free-form mode for an international clientele. Finally, building on his reputation as Brazil's leading architect and leftist champion of his nation's working classes, Niemeyer has emerged today as the master magician of the modernist ritual in Brazilian architecture. Ritual is understood here as a recurring pattern of momentary or localized attempts by elite patrons to address or resolve the country's developmental dilemmas through architectural and urban projects that involve social edification, political indoctrination, popular co-optation, or cultural creation. Niemeyer's architecture of the 1980s and early 1990s fulfills this role while revealing the contradictions of patronage and social intention. His recent works illustrate how his architecture has functioned sometimes as an escape valve for social frustrations, sometimes as a gratification of the whims and political ambitions of elite patrons, and sometimes as both. A freer, surrealist style characterizes these projects: the Memorial da América Latina in São Paulo and the Museu de Arte Contemporânea in Niterói.

Several key architectural undertakings with which Niemeyer has been associated have assumed paramount importance within Brazilian history because they have functioned in a special, but not always obvious, relationship to social critique and transformation, on the one hand, and elite political consolidation, on the other. These projects share certain ritualistic features, such as the attempt to change history through a ground-breaking work of monumental proportions, usually carried out with public funds and completed in record time, and the collaboration of elites of diverse political allegiances willing to bend or even break the rules of society to achieve their goals. Early projects like the ministry building in Rio and the Pampulha complex in Minas Gerais, while important for their formal innovations, take on greater significance as part of this pattern of ritual architecture, which also includes Brasília, the Samba Stadium and the Centros Integrados de Educação Pública (a new public school system) in Rio, and most recently the Memorial da América Latina. Niemeyer has explored more private rituals in such highly personal works as his own house at Canoas, the Ministry of Education theater project, and the project for a new exhibition annex for Ibirapuera, all of which reflect the architect's fascination with the curving forms and feminine mystique of the Brazilian landscape.

The sociopolitical basis of Niemeyer's great archi-rituals is an elite patronage system that demands a monumental architecture of novel forms and outspoken expression. On one level, such work advertises to the masses the achievements of politicians and their commitment to public works (often on the eve of elections) and on another level shows to the world the country's unique cultural identity and "progress" (usually achieved at painful cost to the majority of Brazilians). Ultimately, Niemeyer's architecture is a personal quest for eternity (the architect's and the patron's) and also a larger cultural quest for international recognition. Both are rooted in the elitist assumption, basic to Brazil's ideology of diffusionist development, that giving free reign to certain creative individuals (artists and their patrons) is the best way to achieve development for everyone. Sooner or later, it is argued, the benefits will trickle down to all.

Niemeyer's crucial role in the modernist ideology that sees architecture as motor and symbol of Brazilian national development places him at the center of what anthropologist Roberto Damatta calls "the Brazilian dilemma." A number of cultural and socioeconomic paradoxes have long disturbed Damatta, among them the contrast "between a people so oppressed and a system of personal relationships so preoccupied with personalities and sentiments; between a multitude so faceless and voiceless and an elite so loud in calling for its prerogatives and rights; between an intellectual life so preoccupied with the heart of Brazil, on the one hand, and so attuned to the latest French book on the other; between domestic servants who go unnoticed and employers who are so egocentric."[1] Not surprisingly, Niemeyer's career reflects a set of related contradictions: a Communist architect outspoken in his support of the exploited Brazilian masses yet ready to create vainglorious monuments for the ambitious demagogues who exploit them; a design philosophy attuned to local sources—the intimate warmth and curving sensuality of the tropical Brazilian place—yet committed to a utopian impulse that has engendered vast, cold non-places of reinforced concrete; an extemporized design approach concerned with physical appearances yet preoccupied with the creation of an eternal and ultimately transcendent symbolism; a movement determined to change society through architecture and an architect convinced that architecture can only reflect a society that he cannot change; a sensibility steeped in the notion of liberty and independence and an architecture controlled by a forced and all-encompassing unity.

The central preoccupation of Niemeyer's work has been to harmonize aesthetically the dialectics of modernism, modified and intensified by the contradictions of the Brazilian dilemma. The search for a convincing modernist aesthetic—an obstinate utopia of beauty capable of creatively reconciling such fundamental dichotomies as freedom and control, diversity and unity, art and social action, poetry and technique, the Brazilian and the modern—has been Niemeyer's most fundamental undertaking. His point of departure has been the synthesis of Le Corbusier, whose discourse is itself rooted in what Alan Plattus has called "a dialectical itinerary."[2] Yet rather than accepting modernist formulas wholesale and applying them indiscriminately to the new context, Niemeyer has modified European concepts as the Brazilian context has demanded. Niemeyer's strategies of modernist harmonization are in line with the basic mechanisms of ritualization—inversion, reinforcement, neutralization—that Damatta finds operative in Brazilian society.

Niemeyer's synthesis of modernist oppositions has been fundamentally conditioned by the historical circumstances and physical and socioeconomic contrasts of Brazil. Extremes appear in the country's topography and climate, from the intense tropical heat of the Amazon to the temperate climes of the south; from the dramatic mountains, luxuriant vegetation, and picturesque curving shorelines of Rio's Atlantic coast to the vast, scrubby flatlands of the Brazilian frontier. Contrasts also characterize Brazil's social and economic evolution from an untamed jungle populated by primitive natives and European conquistadors into a patriarchal plantation economy of land barons and African slaves, and then into an emerging industrial giant characterized by the enormous disparity between the haves and the have-nots typical of developing countries. When the Portuguese arrived at the dawn of the Renaissance, Brazil seemed the perfect testing ground for the European humanist assumption that the "civilization" of the new world would quickly follow from the creation of an architecture of churches and fortresses—forms that would either restructure the native society or obliterate it. Thus would arise a new European world in the tropics, a world based on imperial domination and tropical accommodation. When the Luso-Brazilian overlords of the nineteenth and early twentieth centuries brought in French specialists like Grandjean de Montigny, Alfred Agache, and Le Corbusier to civilize Rio de Janeiro by modernizing its architecture, they were in effect trying to finish an old colonial job with new rhetoric and tools. Brazil became the laboratory for the civilizing ideals of the apostles of progress, and then an experimental field in which to prove that architecture could spawn a modernist utopia all too ill-defined, even to those who envisioned it. Niemeyer, in attempting to define this utopia in more Brazilian and aesthetic terms, has had to come to terms with the positivist, Eurocentric, and imperialist underpinnings of modernism and especially with his personal distaste for what he calls "rational architecture." For him, Brazil's artistic identity is synonymous with rejecting a European tendency that has nonetheless laid the foundation for his own structural and spatial conquests in reinforced concrete.

Niemeyer's most important adaptation of the dialectics of modernism concerns the dichotomies of form/function, art/society, and nature/culture. Building on the lyrical element in Le Corbusier's discourse—the Le Corbusier of the *Précisions,* who celebrated the organic contours of the "law of the meander" and translated them into monumental urban form in his 1929 project for Rio—Niemeyer has deemphasized functional considerations and elevated form and visual poetry. Rather than presenting architecture as a surrogate for social reform, as Le Corbusier did with his battle cry "architecture or revolution," Niemeyer sees himself above all as a creator of sculptural forms that echo the curving contours of the tropical landscape and are thus in tune with the mystique of a mythical Nature. The creation of truly Brazilian modern forms must begin with the Brazilian environment, which Niemeyer defines broadly to include not only the physical milieu but also the cultural, socioeconomic, and political domains. Niemeyer's analysis of his Brazilian context has led him to conclude that a responsible "social architecture" is not possible, given the nation's underdevelopment and elite patronage. Moreover, Le Corbusier's definition of architecture as a play of forms brought together in light took on new relevance in the sun-drenched tropics. Both the tropical setting and the country's social dilemmas intensified the dichotomies of Corbusian modernism, setting up more dramatic polarities that in turn have demanded more insistent syntheses, forced unities rooted, paradoxically, in the accentuation of formal contrasts. Niemeyer's architecture is thus a utopian attempt to resolve nonaesthetic problems through formal means. His work has often set out to deny or whitewash the underlying contradictions of the Brazilian dilemma but ended up reflecting, even reinforcing them. In a precarious Third World environment in which, more often than not, things fall apart, Niemeyer has sought an architecture of monumental permanence that projects an image of consolidation—an abstract yet highly ideological art that takes its expressive power as much from a forceful integration of complex functions into volumetric unities defined by formal oppositions as from bold structural innovations made possible by the advanced techniques of reinforced concrete. Because the meaning of this art is rooted in the architect's efforts to deal in aesthetic terms with the nonaesthetic problems of the Brazilian dilemma, discussion must focus on the evolution of Niemeyer's forms and style within the broader sociopolitical context of modern Brazil.

The Corbusian Discourse and the Architecture of Rio

The first phase of Niemeyer's career is characterized by his assimilation, refinement, and creative adaptation of the formal and theoretical discourses of Le Corbusier. Three important buildings in Rio de Janeiro best illustrate this process: the Ministry of Education and Health Building (1936–43), the Obra do Berço (1937), and the architect's own house overlooking the Lagoa Rodrigo de Freitas (1942). The ministry project was the laboratory in which Niemeyer and a team of young Brazilian architects absorbed and refined Corbusian ideas and methods. The Obra do Berço, Niemeyer's first independent project, adapts the purist geometries of Le Corbusier's Citrohan House to a new function: a day nursery for Rio's working mothers. In the Lagoa House, Niemeyer again adapted the Citrohan model and reworked Le Corbusier's five points (pilotis, free plan, free facade, ribbon windows, and roof garden) in a hillside residence that also exploits Brazil's vernacular colonial architecture and evokes the hillside *favelas* (shanties) of Rio de Janeiro. These buildings show that, by the early 1940s, Niemeyer had mastered the basic elements of the Corbusian discourse and begun to move beyond it into more creative transformations that respond directly to Brazilian conditions and needs.

The Ministry of Education and Health Building in Rio de Janeiro Niemeyer's career as an architect dates from his involvement in the project for the Ministry of Education and Health Building in Rio (figs. 6–8), the first work of monumental public architecture in the Corbusian style to be officially sanctioned and erected by a Latin American government. Commissioned by President Getúlio Vargas's ambitious and reforming minister of education, Gustavo Capanema, the building illustrates both the search for new cultural symbols and the appropriation of modernist forms fostered by the authoritarian government that came to power in Brazil's 1930 revolution. The building is the complex product of a fruitful artistic and technical collaboration between Le Corbusier and a talented team of architects and artists headed by Lúcio Costa and Niemeyer. The project's innovative application and refinement of the five-points and brise-soleil systems pioneered the adaptation of Corbusian forms to a tropical context. The building spearheaded the acceptance of Corbusian modernism in Latin America and served as a model of creative assimilation for the rest of the world, at a time when public buildings in Europe and America were still being designed in the classical style. The ministry was the prototype of the concrete slab office tower with an urban plaza, later developed by Niemeyer in the United Nations complex in New York.[1]

Capanema was determined to create an epoch-making building

6. Le Corbusier, Lúcio Costa, Niemeyer, et al.,
Ministry of Education and Health Building,
Rio de Janeiro, 1936–43, north facade

7. Le Corbusier, Lúcio Costa, Niemeyer, et al.,
Ministry of Education and Health Building,
Rio de Janeiro, 1936–43, north facade

8. Le Corbusier, Lúcio Costa, Niemeyer, et al.,
Ministry of Education and Health Building,
Rio de Janeiro, 1936–43, south facade

that would symbolize the modernizing aspirations of the new regime. Dissatisfied with the academic and historicist entries selected in a design competition held in 1935, Capanema, who presided over a jury of academicists, paid the winners their cash prizes and called upon Costa to come up with a new, modernist solution that would move Brazil into the mainstream of the International Style.[2] This arbitrary action, though initially stirring outrage, was gradually accepted, in part because of increasing public recognition that Costa, who had initiated the curricular reform of Rio's Escola Nacional de Belas Artes in 1930–31, was the undisputed leader of the new generation of Brazilian architects. Capanema had also managed to convince Vargas to pass a law stating that the ministry project should be an exception to the rule that all design projects for public buildings had to pass through an open competition before gaining official approval.[3] Modern architectural innovation in Brazil was the stepchild of authoritarian politics and the *jeito brasileiro*—the special Brazilian trick of "solving" problems by going around them.

Costa, perceiving Capanema's solicitation as a triumph for the modernist cause rather than as a personal victory, accepted the invitation on the condition that several of the young architects under his wing—Carlos Leão, Affonso Reidy, and Jorge Moreira—be allowed to collaborate with him on the design. To this group would be added two others: Ernani Vasconcelos, at the insistence of Moreira, his usual collaborator, and Niemeyer, who, determined not to be left out, demanded that he be allowed to participate because of his position as Costa's chief draftsman. This definitive design team, formed in early 1936, was highly homogeneous: all were students of the reformed fine arts academy, and all were committed to Le Corbusier's principles.

This commitment was reinforced by intimate personal contact with the European master, which occurred during Le Corbusier's six-week stay in Rio beginning in July 1936. Convinced that the best way to produce an avant-garde building was to go straight to its European source, Capanema invited Le Corbusier to consult on the design of the ministry, submit a plan for the *cidade universitária* (university city), and deliver a series of conferences on architecture.[4] Le Corbusier soon assumed leadership over the initial planning of the ministry.

In this auspicious context Niemeyer made his debut on Rio's architectural scene. Before 1936, he had worked only as an assistant and draftsman in the office of Costa and Leão, where he revealed little distinction beyond an exceptional determination to succeed. He had entered Costa's office as a volunteer and for some time accepted no payment for his services. Costa recalls that Niemeyer

revealed only after Le Corbusier's visit to Brazil."[5] The ministry project, which offered Niemeyer direct exposure to Le Corbusier, was the key formative episode in his development as an architect, introducing him to the practical aspects of Corbusian design in a concrete application of the architect's theories. Thus Niemeyer experimented and became comfortable with the magical methods and ingredients of the Corbusian discourse. He observed firsthand Le Corbusier's forceful personality, intellectual integrity, informal approach, and spontaneous sketching method, which Niemeyer mastered by tracing the master's drawings. He also experienced the application of the five points to a monumental office slab, the valorization of architecture as a plastic art, the preoccupation with formal matters, and the sensitivity to local conditions, from the tropical climate to the artistic legacy of colonial Brazil. In Le Corbusier, Niemeyer observed a vital and highly effective synthesis of freedom and authority, which became a hallmark of his own work.

Le Corbusier's major contribution to the development of Brazilian modernism consisted in moving the Brazilians away from certain academic tendencies of early Brazilian functionalism, such as the rigidly symmetrical U-shaped plan initially proposed by Costa's team. Le Corbusier thereby opened the door to greater freedom and experimentation in design. The ministry reflects two separate artistic processes: the replacement of the beaux-arts-inspired approaches of the first Brazilian proposals by a freer Corbusian aesthetic based on a sweeping horizontal monolith with asymmetrically disposed masses, and the

9, 10. Le Corbusier,
first (top) and second (bottom) projects for the
Ministry of Education and Health Building,
Rio de Janeiro, 1936

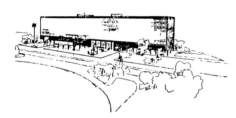

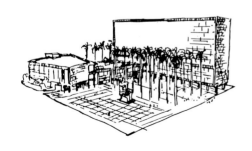

Brazilian refinement of the Corbusian solution adopted, which created a lighter, more airy, taller structure highly adaptable to the local climate. Building upon Le Corbusier's innovative planning but rejecting his first proposal for a waterfront site on the Praia Santa Luzia (fig. 9), the team elaborated its design from his second project, dated August 13, 1936, for a site in the Castelo business district (fig. 10). This second project introduced a plaza that interacted dynamically with the street pattern of the center-city lot.

Le Corbusier's proposal for a horizontal composition of three distinct volumes—the principal office block, the exposition salon (perpendicular to the main block), and the conference salon (across from the exposition salon)—was carefully modified by the Brazilian team into a more vertical solution of two perpendicular volumes. This new T-plan, achieved by placing the exposition and conference salons on the same axis, resulted in a more unified and integrated composition. The main block and exposition wing thus intersect at the conference salon, which lies on the

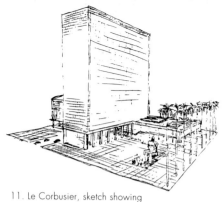

11. Le Corbusier, sketch showing
definitive development of the
Ministry of Education and Health Building,
Rio de Janeiro, 1937

ground floor. Its height demanded that the pilotis of the main block be increased in height from Le Corbusier's proposed four meters to ten, so that the intersection of the two wings would be visually and volumetrically congruous.

The team's taller slab, elevated on these taller and more slender pilotis, led to a more dynamic and floating solution. In the exposition wing, by contrast, the pilotis were moved outward from the body of the structure and conceived as columns that support their superstructures with small consoles or brackets of reinforced concrete. The result is a daring sense of structural lightness that became the hallmark of Niemeyer's work. His influence seems equally evident in the incorporation of complex functions into a unified volume. In 1940 Costa resigned as chief architect and left the direction of the team to Niemeyer, whose impact on the plastic conception of the ensemble had by that time become dominant.

Niemeyer played the major role in refining the design's Corbusian ideas. After Le Corbusier left for France on August 18, the Brazilians continued to effect minor alterations and refinements to the second, Castelo project, completing work several months later. Leão relates that one December morning Niemeyer appeared in his office with a set of designs that he had been developing on his own in his spare time. The drawings deeply impressed Leão for their creative assimilation of Corbusian principles. When Costa arrived, Niemeyer grabbed the drawings and threw them out the window, fearing that Costa would think him insolent for working alone on a new project, but Leão demanded that Niemeyer show them to Costa. A subtle and balanced modification of Le Corbusier's Castelo project, incorporating elements of the proposal for the first, Santa Luzia site, Niemeyer's project became the pilot plan for the final design.[6] On January 5, 1937, his project was officially presented in professional Corbusian manner, with a perspective showing an eleven-story prism elevated on ten-meter pilotis, set in an urban landscape with imperial palms, people, cars, and Celso Antonio's monumental sculpture *O Homen Brasileiro*.[7] The impact of the refinements introduced by Niemeyer and the Brazilian team can be seen in a sketch of the definitive design drawn by Le Corbusier in 1937, based on the final project that Costa sent to Le Corbusier in France (fig. 11).[8]

12. Le Corbusier, Lúcio Costa, Niemeyer, et al.,
Ministry of Education and Health Building,
Rio de Janeiro, 1936–43, *quebra sol* on north
facade

The adjustable brise-soleils on the ministry's north facade also appear to have been Niemeyer's idea. In 1933 housing projects for Barcelona and Algiers, Le Corbusier had proposed a brise-soleil in the form of a fixed concrete grid on the facades. The first Brazilian example of a fixed brise-soleil appears on the

13. Marcelo and Milton Ribeiro,
A.B.I. Building (Associação Brasileira da Imprensa),
Rio de Janeiro, 1936–38

A.B.I. Building in Rio (1936), designed with vertical panels, by the brothers Marcelo and Milton Ribeiro (fig. 13). The variant used on the ministry, however, is a horizontal *quebra sol*, a system of movable louvers that can adjust individually, from inside the building, in accordance with the changing angle of the sun and the flow of maritime breezes (fig. 12). Niemeyer's first independent work, the Obra do Berço, first presented this device. Later he pointed out its advantages: "Considering the changing direction of solar rays in relation to the facade, the best system for obstructing them is that of movable panels."[9] Beyond functional advantages, the *quebra sol* system applied across the north facade visually balances horizontal elements and the vertical block and increases the plastic effect and compositional interest deriving from the richer and more varied play of light and shade. The *quebra sol* dissatisfied Le Corbusier, however, who felt that no one should tamper with his advanced technical system. Niemeyer seemed to proclaim the freedom of the individual to make his own adjustments to a rigid system that for him came to symbolize the standardized banality of European rational architecture. Much to Le Corbusier's dismay and delight, Niemeyer's minor adjustments would soon become major iconoclasms.

The final plan for the ministry also reflects Le Corbusier's desire to create a harmonious architectural ensemble that integrated all plastic arts in a multimedia project showcasing Brazil's native talents. He encouraged the team to integrate local traditions and materials such as *carioca* (native to Rio) gneiss and *azulejos* (decorative ceramic tiles) for textural variety and to include tropical landscaping and a sculptural centerpiece to focus the multimedia architectural symphony. Yet the evolution of the design and the building as executed illustrate that the Brazilian team went well beyond Le Corbusier's suggestions to create their own masterpiece, one that would advertise the progress of Brazilian modernism internationally. The overall impact of the modifications to Le Corbusier's original proposals is a plastically richer work that is both more monumental and more dynamic, with greater emphasis on formal lyricism and decorative exuberance. The colorful *azulejo* wall panels by Candido Portinari; the sculptures of Bruno Giorgi, Antonio Celso, and Jacques Lipschitz; and the landscape gardening of Roberto Burle Marx mark the building as a milestone in Brazilian artistic collaboration.[10] The project thus gave rise to a new school of Brazilian artists and engendered a collaborative spirit that would mark the evolution of modernism in Brazil. The ministry is the first chapter in a long story whose major protagonists—Costa, Niemeyer, Burle Marx, and Portinari—frequently reappear.

The ministry project demonstrates the importance of forceful state patronage in sponsoring modernist innovation in architecture and reveals how the new architecture became identified with state intentions, serving as both symbol of a new techno-industrial order and aesthetic model to promote and advertise national development. Modernist architecture in São Paulo had not gained widespread acceptance because its backers were mostly private patrons. But because of the enlightened public interest and political ambition of a handful of government patrons like Vargas and Capanema, who, foreshadowing the patronage of Juscelino Kubitschek, Orestes Quércia, and Leonel Brizola, saw the potential power of architecture as a maker and marker of a new national culture, the emergence of modern architecture in Brazil would be synonymous with the architectural development of Brazil's capital cities (federal and state): first Rio de Janeiro and Belo Horizonte, later Brasília and São Paulo.

The Ministry of Education and Health Building was from its inception part of a larger effort to create a new cultural and sociopolitical tradition for Brazil through architecture. It thus partook of Le Corbusier's reformist zeal by evoking a streamlined, hygienic, and efficient bureaucracy of positivist technocrats that would lead Brazil into an industrialized future. As a palace of the arts, it sought to project an image of Brazil's modernity to the rest of the world. The creation of the building thus inaugurated a new ritual—a modern tradition of political, artistic, and intellectual collaboration in which a small group of powerful individuals seek to change history through a ground-breaking architectural project carried out under adverse circumstances—in this case, the lack of skilled labor and industrial capabilities, the political upheaval of 1937 (Vargas suspended Brazil's constitution and inaugurated the dictatorial Estado Novo), and a world war. The ministry is the first modern Brazilian building to celebrate the heroic Corbusian ideal of public man as agent of change in an otherwise tragic historical destiny. This ritual would be reenacted often throughout Niemeyer's career.

The ministry building established a number of important precedents, among them the architect's right to innovate in the face of a stagnant political and cultural system too long tied to traditional interests. Several years after the completion of the building, Costa observed that the decision not to build the project that had won the competition was "a lesson and a warning because it seemed to insinuate that when the normal state of things is one of organized sickness, and the error lies in the law, the breaking of the norm imposes itself and illegality is fruitful."[11] Such statements seem to sanction Niemeyer's subsequent architectural innovations openly.

The building was perceived locally as an extravagant "palace of luxury." The arrival in 1942 of Phillip Goodwin and G. E. Kidder-Smith, however, precipitated a change in public opinion. Goodwin, visiting Brazil to collect material for the Museum of Modern Art's exhibition on Brazilian architecture,

14. Niemeyer,
Obra do Berço (day nursery), Rio de Janeiro,
1937

15. Niemeyer,
Obra do Berço, Rio de Janeiro, 1937, plans

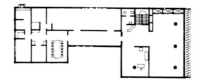

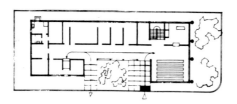

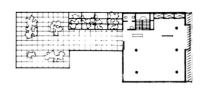

called the ministry "the most advanced building in the Americas."[12] Critics, both foreign and Brazilian, were much impressed with its Brazilian qualities and the manner in which it exemplified the skillful adaptation of European ideas. As Italo Campofiorito wrote: "The Ministry . . . is an extremely youthful building, with a lightness of touch to its proportions, a 'jeito' brasileiro that demonstrates, to those who can understand, that the final project, although inspired by Le Corbusier, is native to Brazil."[13]

Although Niemeyer submitted the final design and was responsible for a number of its refinements and the furniture, he does not think of the work as his. His first building, he claims, is the Obra do Berço.

The Obra do Berço in Rio de Janeiro The Obra do Berço (fig. 14), Niemeyer's first independent built work, adapts the Corbusian discourse of purist volumes and the five points in a new social welfare institution created by the federal government to assist Rio's working classes. Its program, which included a day nursery, a health clinic, and facilities for dispensing free milk to poor mothers, reflects the paternalist benevolence of the demagogic regime instituted by Getúlio Vargas in 1937. The Berço reveals the new state's sponsorship of Niemeyer and the uses of his architecture in Brazil's modernization.

A modification of the Citrohan House cube for a new (public) function, the building demonstrates Niemeyer's ability to monumentalize a Corbusian theme and impose an appropriately authoritarian sense of abstract formal unity on a building with a complex program. The building's binuclear plan resembles that of Frank Lloyd Wright's Unity Temple—an arrangement typical of early functionalism in Europe and America. The Berço is composed of two cubes, one of three and one of four stories, linked by a rectangular, two-story "bridge" (fig. 15). On the ground floor, this bridge contains a reception gallery separated from the exterior entrance patio only by a low concrete wall carrying four slender pilotis, which read as the columns of a porch (fig. 17). Echoing the colonnaded veranda of the colonial Brazilian plantation house, this space conveys an open, welcoming feeling and provides a subtle transition between exterior and interior. The gallery connects the entrance and main waiting room in the front (four-story) block to the small examination and milk preparation rooms in the rear block. This spatial fluidity and abstract evocation of a vernacular theme make the building seem accessible and familiar to the workers who must enter it to receive handouts from the all-powerful state.

Compared to the gallery, however, the main rooms seem cramped. The plan grows more fluid and spacious as one ascends the architectural (and social) hierarchy. Preferential spatial treatment is given to a large multipurpose room with movable partitions located on the top floor of the main block, as well as to the spacious lounge just beneath it on the third story. The lounge opens onto a sizable garden that stretches back onto the roof of the rear block. On the second floor, the director's office and sewing room in the front block seem disproportionately large compared to the constricted rectangle of the main nursery room, which extends back along the axis of the bridge to connect with the very small dining room and nurses' station. As in buildings for the elite, with spacious penthouses and ocean-view living rooms, the most ample spaces in the Berço are in front and on top. The spaces in the rear block and connecting wing seem inadequate to the needs of an emerging welfare state. After the facility was inaugurated, the gallery became an overflow waiting area. Niemeyer and his government patrons seem to have underestimated the dimensions of Brazil's poverty.

The building's design reflects the dialectic of Brazilian development in its two facades—one imposing, monumental, official, and Corbusian (on the west side, toward the Lagoa Rodrigo de Freitas) and one popular, more open and accessible on the street level, and imbued with the Brazilian vernacular (on the north). Niemeyer originally designed a horizontal *quebra sol* for the west facade, but when it proved ineffective against the strong tropical sun, intensified by the glare reflected off the lake, the architect removed it and installed the extant vertical panels at his own expense (fig. 16). These vertical louvers, the first adjustable brise-soleil in Brazil, brought a felicitous and somewhat unanticipated aesthetic result: the prevailing horizontals of the old panels and their white concrete frames were replaced by a contrasting linear pattern that better balanced horizontal and vertical. The new louvers also increase the vertical thrust of the whole by continuing the lines of the tall pilotis supporting the cube. The new arrangement thus results in a livelier, more balanced, monumental facade that also functions more effectively.

The case of the replaced *quebra sol* in the Obra do Berço illustrates Niemeyer's personal commitment to improvement and his willingness to extemporize—in this instance, after the building was finished—to find solutions that work better in a tropical environment. At the Berço, Niemeyer may also have been responding to the political priorities of the Vargas government. The adaptation of Citrohan House cubes and colonial verandas to a public building architecturally domesticates both the government workplace—in this case, a new bureaucratic institution of the demagogic corporatist regime—and the working classes which such institutions were designed (in theory) to serve, and (in practice) to control. Le Corbusier's dictum "architecture or revolution" implied that revolution could be averted by attending to the working-class housing problem. Housing was only part of the problem, though, and in Brazil it was a

16. Niemeyer,
Obra do Berço, Rio de Janeiro, 1937,
main facade with *quebra sol*

17 (overleaf). Niemeyer,
Obra do Berço, Rio de Janeiro, 1937,
entrance gallery

18. Niemeyer,
Niemeyer House (Lagoa House), near the Lagoa
Rodrigo de Freitas, Rio de Janeiro, 1942

19. Niemeyer,
Lagoa House, Rio de Janeiro, 1942, section and
floor plan

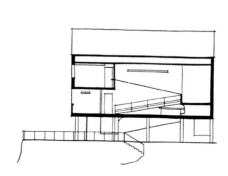

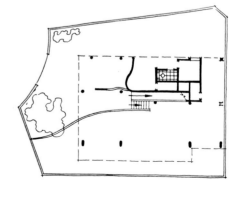

problem about which the state cared little. However, the Vargas regime, in need of legitimizing its power after suspending basic constitutional rights, did have an interest in finding architectural forms that projected an image of paternalist benevolence and accessibility, especially forms that satisfied the elite's desire for a modern style while appealing to lower classes conditioned by the patriarchal control and class relations associated with the image and institution of the colonial plantation house. One way to guarantee the corporatist pact and ensure popular support was to create benevolent public institutions like the Berço, which presented both an accessible, "popular" face and a monumental, official image of state power. Modern architecture in Brazil, and Niemeyer's in particular, has often been an effective tool for popular co-optation, what Youssef Cohen calls "the manipulation of consent."[14]

Since colonial times, domestic architecture as a microcosm of Portuguese society and the domestication or privatization of the public realm have been central to the culture and political relations of the Portuguese and Brazilian peoples.[15] Niemeyer's own house exemplifies this point while illustrating the next stage in his ongoing tropical adaptation of the Corbusian discourse.

The Niemeyer House on the Lagoa Rodrigo de Freitas in Rio de Janeiro The house that Niemeyer designed for himself in 1942 in the Lagoa section of Rio de Janeiro (figs. 18, 19) exemplifies the self-serving attitude of Brazil's governing elite toward the country's housing crisis. With its cramped service quarters below and spacious living spaces above, the house is not only a barometer of the persistence of traditional social hierarchies but also an excellent gauge of the architect's feelings about himself and his architecture. The houses architects design for themselves are as much personal playgrounds as residences, and here Niemeyer plays some of his favorite design games as he strives to create a new symbolic unity based on the symbiosis of the discourses of Le Corbusier and Rio de Janeiro.

The Lagoa house is also an excellent example of Niemeyer's adaptive synthesis of the Corbusian five points and vernacular traditions of his native Rio. Erected on a steep escarpment overlooking the Lagoa Rodrigo de Freitas, not far from the Obra do Berço, the house has pilotis, a free plan, and a free facade with modified ribbon windows. The architect again took up the theme of Le Corbusier's Citrohan House—a reinforced concrete cube with a split-level living room—and modified it, according to Brazilian colonial practice, with a broad, partially covered veranda; white stucco walls; a single-pitch, red-tile roof; and blue wooden blinds. Niemeyer's *carioca* interpretation of a Corbusian theme thus relieves the heavy purist monotony of the white Citrohan cube with vernacular color and texture and a

20. **Favela,** Rio de Janeiro

tropical airiness, structural lightness, and monumental elegance—the three most characteristic features of his new Brazilian modernism.

To a large extent these three qualities result from the structural system of thin pilotis, which enabled the architect to create an open but compact plan that maximizes the amount of usable space on the cramped, sloped site. The economic and topographical advantages of the piloti construction system were even more compelling and practical for *cariocas* than they were in the European milieu or in Le Corbusier's abstract theoretical system. Using pilotis meant that the terrain could be left substantially unprepared; the cost of construction on hillside sites dropped because expensive grading and elaborate foundations became unnecessary. The pilotis also elevate the dwelling, freeing it from the limitations of the site and providing the architect with a commanding view of nature, lake, and city below.

Niemeyer's use of ramps instead of stairs to create an interior procession that culminates in the dramatic view from the living room reflects his interest in controlling shifting visual perspectives from above. From its privileged physical (and moral) position, high above the clamor of the city and the street, the Lagoa House celebrates the values of privacy, individual freedom, and visual domination that are so important to Niemeyer as an artist and as a person.

As with the *quebra sol* systems of the ministry and Berço, Niemeyer's house adapts the new architecture to local environmental conditions. Niemeyer integrated the house with its natural surroundings in a way that went beyond Le Corbusier's visual framing of nature and artificial re-creation of it in the Citrohan roof garden. The Lagoa House has a garden on the ground level rather than on the roof. Aside from fostering a more organic link between the house and its site, this arrangement has a number of practical advantages. First, the cultivation of the slope around and beneath the house helps secure its topsoil from mud slides and runoff accompanying tropical rains, thus reinforcing the building's natural foundation. Second, it frees the roof, with its projecting eaves, to function as it should in a tropical climate: to throw rainwater away from the house and down the hill.

More than a synthesis of the Corbusian and the local, Niemeyer's house is also a typically *carioca* solution to Rio's perennial housing problem—and is, in certain ways, drawn from an earlier popular solution, the *favela*, or shanty. The city's unique topography of thin, curving coastlines and rugged mountainous terrain had, since colonial times, forced the city's inhabitants into a narrow fringe of land hemmed in between the mountains of the Serra do Mar and the sea. The resulting shortage of space for urban development was intensified by industrialization and the Haussmannization of Rio in the late nineteenth and early twentieth centuries, when the demolition of scores of tenement houses in central Rio forced the lower classes to climb the hills. Evicted from the monumental center, the poor started erecting makeshift wooden shanties and eventually entire *favelas* on the steeper or more peripheral sites left undeveloped by the elite (fig. 20). For the *favelados* these undeveloped hillside sites had certain natural advantages—the free circulation of air from maritime breezes, the dramatic view of the sea, the freedom of movement up and down the hills. For all of their inadequacies and disadvantages, the hillside shanties brought the *favelados* mobility and freedom—spatial and spiritual—that they could not find in the social world of the modern city below. The urban underclass's spatial conquest of the idealized realm of the hills—a highly self-reliant form of social action—substituted for their social participation in the world of modern capitalism. The *favelados* may have been excluded down below, but they gained individual liberty and the most spectacular view of the *cidade maravilhosa* (marvelous city) and the bay.

Niemeyer was certainly aware of this *carioca* discourse of the *favela* as an ideal realm high above the degeneration of street and city, a myth forcefully promoted by Le Corbusier. Echoing Abbé Marc-Antoine Laugier's admiration of the noble savage and the "natural processes" that created the rustic hut of primitive man, Le Corbusier celebrated the "primitive purity" of the blacks in the shanties and saw in their experience the basis for a new modern style rooted in freedom, moral integrity, and a happy life in communion with a magnificent nature. In the American Prologue to *Précisions,* he describes the music of the "simple naive black" as the "basis of a style capable of being the expression of the feelings of a new time," capable of breaking academic European tradition and finding "new explorations. Pure music." Le Corbusier contrasts the "true" naked individual with the false society individual of Europe and the academies. He describes the time he "climbed the hills inhabited by the blacks" and found them "basically *good:* good-hearted. Then beautiful, magnificent." But he was most impressed with "their carelessness, the limits they had learned to impose on their needs, their capacity for dreaming, and their candidness," which resulted in their houses "being always admirably sited, the windows opening astonishingly on magnificent spaces, the smallness of their rooms largely adequate."[16]

From this experience of Rio's *favelas* and *favelados,* Le Corbusier extrapolated an important lesson for modern architecture: "It is the concept of life that must change; it is the concept of happiness that must be made clear."[17] Le Corbusier's ascent to the *favela* (in popular parlance, *a subida do morro*) was a momentous *promenade architecturale:* as he climbed, the dramatic unfolding of shifting views and new perspectives informed him of the magnificent architecture of nature, of Rio's rich spatial symphony and uplifting effect on the human spirit. This experience instigated a major shift in Le Corbusier's thinking from a mechanistic to an organic approach to architecture. Vividly recorded in the lyrical exaltations of the *Précisions*, this outlook was shared by the young Niemeyer, whose Lagoa House shows that he too wanted a house with a view and that he was as conversant in the natural discourse of Rio as in the discourse of Le Corbusier.

Partaking of this modernist ideology, patronizing and romantically idealizing in its attitude toward Afro-Brazilians and the lower classes in general, and especially toward their "carefree" lifestyle in the hillside shanties, Niemeyer's house may thus be understood as a modern "monumentalization of the vernacular"—the transformation of a popular type into a *maison type* for modern Brazil, but one that would serve only the upper classes. The Lagoa House thus reflects the elite's usurpation of the popular tradition of the *subida do morro* (climbing the hills to get home). Thus, the house serves to legitimize the elite conquest of the usual realm of the *favelados* by reference to a popular or vernacular image that conveys a sense of social solidarity or unity across the classes. But in appropriating the tradition of the *favela* and the *subida do morro*, Niemeyer's house aesthetically elevates this solution into the realm of high modernist art for the elite.

The legitimacy of the Lagoa House as a new cultural symbol for modern Brazil thus lies in its fluency with both the high modernist discourse of Le Corbusier and the local *carioca* discourse of the hillside house. By appropriating and synthesizing both these discourses, Niemeyer gives his house a pedigree that is both modernist and Brazilian.

Niemeyer's first mature house is thus a creative harmonization of dialectical categories that recur throughout his career: (1) the ideal and the real (while deriving a real Brazilian house from a Corbusian ideal or theoretical model, the house also abstracts and idealizes a real Brazilian prototype, the hillside shanty); (2) the Corbusian and the Brazilian (while recasting Brazilian tradition in terms of a Corbusian formal system, the design also Brazilianizes Corbusian vocabulary); (3) the universal and the local (while transforming a "universal" five-points system into an authentically local artifact, the house also abstracts and universalizes a set of local traditions); (4) the monumental and the humble, or high and low art (while monumentalizing the humble and the vernacular, the design humbles or popularizes monumental or high Corbusian art); and (5) the traditional and the modern (while modernizing the traditional or vernacular, the house creates a new Brazilian tradition of the modern, a *carioca* house type). As we add to this

21, 22. Niemeyer,
project for a theater for the
Ministry of Education and Health Building,
Rio de Janeiro, 1948, photomontage and section

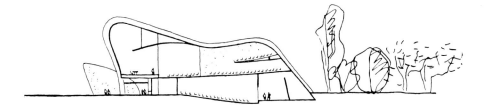

23. Niemeyer,
drawing for "Poem of the Curve," ink and watercolor

list, we will find that Niemeyer's works make use of three major strategies of modernist harmonization: inversion, reinforcement, and neutralization.

In the Lagoa House, Niemeyer basically reinforced Le Corbusier's five points, but inverted the position of the garden. In so doing he took a first step toward neutralizing the Corbusian mechanistic distinction between the building as work of art and nature as something to be artificially contained, framed, or controlled. Niemeyer would not fully synthesize building and *natural* nature until the free-form house at Canoas in the early 1950s.

The Theater Project for the Ministry of Education and Health Building in Rio de Janeiro Niemeyer grew increasingly critical of the rational European design that was his early diet as an architect, and the shift in attitude is fully evident in an important project associated with the Ministry of Education and Health Building: an unbuilt 1948 design for a curvilinear theater with double auditoriums (fig. 21). As the photomontage prepared for the project reveals, the structure was to adjoin the main block of the ministry building on the south side, via a covered walkway or canopy consisting of a concrete slab resting on two rows of tall, thin pilotis. The proposal, with its dramatically suspended ceiling and cantilevered balcony (fig. 22), suggests a new direction for Niemeyer's architecture, in which organic plasticity, structural dynamism, and the play of formal contrasts become the focus. On the one hand is the contrast between the sculptural plasticity of the thin concrete shell and the smooth glazing of Le Corbusier's *pan de verre* (glazed curtain wall) on the south facade. More basic is the contrast between the dynamically curving biomorphic theater and the rigid rectilinearity of Le Corbusier's Cartesian grid. Here Niemeyer seems to protest the rational architecture of the ministry slab. The artistic identity of Brazil lies in the sensual curve suggesting waves washing ashore.

The theater project also reveals Niemeyer's interest in baroque scenography and the control of sight lines. The low, undulating theater literally "sets up" the ministry building from the low visual vantage point of the pedestrian on the street, who is invited to consider the contrast between a biomorphic Brazilian form and the massive, machinelike monumentality of the main block, with its associations with European discipline and official order.

Niemeyer's free-form sketches of the sight lines over the theater (fig. 24) bring to mind a special Rio perspective: that of the beachgoer who contemplates the Copacabana apartment buildings over the curving backsides of sun-tanned *cariocas*. The rippled lines of the roof's structural ribs spread out like legs, recalling Niemeyer's sketches of Brazilian women. The roof lines suggest the contours of a row of female bodies stretched out on their stomachs, sunning their backs. Typical of Niemeyer's formal inversions and interest in sensual, even sexual imagery is his proposal that we approach the very erect, rigid, even masculine ministry building from such a view.

Niemeyer's undulating theater marks the new wave of Brazilian design; it is the visual counterpart to his own explanation of the deepest sources of his architecture. In answer to Le Corbusier's "law of the meander" and "Poem of the Right Angle,"[18] Niemeyer created his "Poem of the Curve" (fig. 23):

It is not the right angle that attracts me, nor the straight line—hard and inflexible—created by man. What attracts me is the free and sensual curve, the curve that I find in the mountains of my country, in the sinuous course of its rivers, in the body of the beloved woman. The entire universe is made of curves, the curved universe of Einstein.[19]

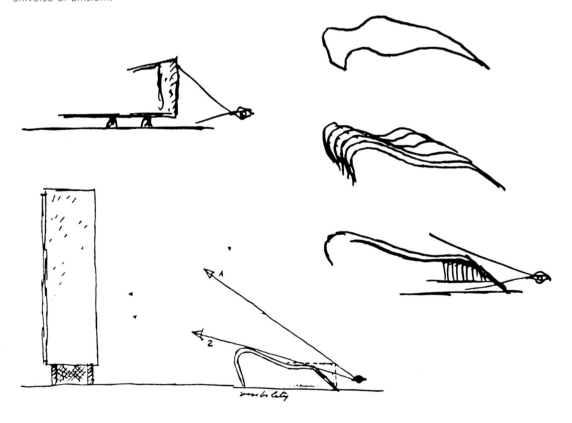

24. Niemeyer,
project for a theater for the
Ministry of Education and Health Building,
Rio de Janeiro, 1948, preliminary sketches showing
sight lines

Free-Form Modernism

While the European rationalists from Gropius to Le Corbusier had sought a sober, hard-lined architecture based on the machine aesthetic, with its mass-produced materials and standardized forms, Niemeyer proclaimed a new Brazilian aesthetic based on the physical geography of Brazil and the suggestion that "form follows feminine."[1] The theater project for the Ministry of Education and Health Building was not the first indication that Niemeyer was moving in the direction of a freer, more plastic architecture derived from his beloved Brazilian curve. The initial full-scale development of his free-form ideas came as early as 1938–39, when he collaborated with Lúcio Costa on the challenging project for the Brazilian Pavilion for the New York World's Fair. The pavilion opened a new chapter in Niemeyer's career and in the history of Brazilian modernism, bringing international recognition to both. Whereas the ministry, Berço, and Lagoa House essentially involve refinements and adaptations of Le Corbusier's formal language, the Brazilian Pavilion, the buildings at Pampulha, and his own Canoas House move beyond formal vocabulary to develop, in curvilinear Brazilian forms, some of the most important Corbusian design concepts—the free plan, the *marriage de contour* (marriage of contours), the *promenade architecturale* (architectural promenade), and the *jeu de rampes* (play of ramps).

In these works Niemeyer began to play his favorite game, formal inversion. The Brazilian Pavilion and Pampulha complex anticipate the neutralized distinction between nature and architecture worked out more fully at Canoas, where the inversion of architectural conventions reaches new proportions. In all of these works, landscape and site are Niemeyer's points of departure for free-form compositions. Architecture evolves from a multidimensional frame for the visual experience of nature into something much more harmoniously, even organically integrated with it. In Canoas the lush tropical landscape of Brazil begins to overtake and entangle the analytic clarity of modern categories.

The Brazilian Pavilion at the New York World's Fair The Brazilian Pavilion at the New York World's Fair of 1939–40 (fig. 27) is the first independent statement of Brazilian modernism.[2] By developing a number of important themes that would recur in Niemeyer's work, the pavilion prepared the way for Pampulha and Canoas, the masterworks of Niemeyer's free-form modernism. Bringing the free plan to a new level of fluidity and spatial interpenetration, the building reflects a more complete Brazilianization of the International Style and Corbusian ideas. The contours of the site and the view of the landscape, natural and constructed, became major elements in the design.

Niemeyer here again adopted the five-points system but brought the roof garden

25. Lúcio Costa and Niemeyer,
**Brazilian Pavilion for New York World's
Fair,** 1939, lily pond and glazed facade

26. Lúcio Costa and Niemeyer,
**Brazilian Pavilion for New York World's
Fair,** 1939, glazed facade facing interior court

27. Lúcio Costa and Niemeyer,
**Brazilian Pavilion for New York World's
Fair,** 1939, main facade

down to earth, as in the Lagoa House. The pavilion's "natural" milieu was entirely built, consisting of a water-lily pond, orchid house, snake pit, and aquarium—all integrated into a lush garden that graced the middle of the chilly New York fairgrounds with a taste of tropical paradise (fig. 25). The plastic concept of the building as an open-air pavilion planned around a pond and garden court with tropical flora and fauna successfully exploits the Corbusian concepts of the *marriage de contour* and the *promenade architecturale* in a spirited and seductively inviting evocation of the exuberant landscape of Rio de Janeiro.

The Brazilian Pavilion, compared with its International Style prototype, Mies van der Rohe's German pavilion in Barcelona of 1929, another asymmetrical composition arranged around a pool with a dynamic spatial fluidity made possible by new structural techniques, uniquely expressed a national culture in the making rather than an abstract, universal statement of technological and material refinement. Whereas the Barcelona Pavilion is all straight lines and de Stijl, the Brazilian Pavilion combined the controlled spatial progression of the Corbusian manner with the curvilinear *jeito* of Brazil. The play of water and curving contours, which created a graceful equilibrium of undulating rhythms, are a major ingredient of Niemeyer's mature style and a key element in this design. The architect achieved spatial fluidity and understated elegance with extensive glazing and inexpensive, industrially produced steel frame materials appropriate for a temporary exposition structure (fig. 26). The Brazilian Pavilion was thus a compromise between the International Style, with its preference for steel construction, and the more sculptural aspirations of Brazilian designers, who would have shed the steel frame and let the concrete pour forth more freely, as it would in Niemeyer's later work. Costa and Niemeyer encased the steel I-beams of the building's structure in a curved, plate-metal sheathing that echoes the free-form composition.

The project for the World's Fair originated in a 1938 competition sponsored by the Brazilian Ministry of Labor. The jury was composed of ministry officials and architects from the Instituto de Arquitetos do Brasil. Submissions were judged according to how well they expressed Brazil's national character and how well they met the needs of a temporary pavilion for an exposition with the futurist theme "The World of Tomorrow."[3] This dual requirement suggested an architectural definition of national character leaning more toward "what a Brazilian building wants to be" than toward the habitual imitation of past forms that had characterized Brazil's neocolonial contributions to previous international expositions, such as the one held in Philadelphia in 1926. The jury's new criteria demanded no less than the immediate creation of the first completely modern, completely Brazilian building.

28. Lúcio Costa and Niemeyer,
**Brazilian Pavilion for New York World's
Fair,** 1939, drawing

This was a large order to fill for Brazil's nascent modernists, who had only begun to define themselves in relation to the International Style but had not yet freed themselves from the Corbusian system. As Yves Bruand has pointed out, mature reflection, not spontaneous extemporization, was needed to meet the twin requirements; the jury members were dissatisfied with all of the submissions.[4] The project by Costa, the staunchest supporter of Brazilian character in architecture, placed first, and Niemeyer's second. Yet Costa was so impressed with Niemeyer's project that he asked the jury to allow him to collaborate with Niemeyer on a new one. Costa's generous attitude, expressed three years earlier in the Ministry of Education and Health project, reflected the cultured and modest personality of a man genuinely and idealistically committed to the larger goal of creating a better architecture for Brazil. Convinced, as was Le Corbusier, that architecture was above all a sculptural art, Costa appreciated Niemeyer's plastic inventiveness and encouraged his innovations for Brazil's modernist cause. Niemeyer's rapid rise thus owes much to Costa's continual support; the latter gave Niemeyer every chance to express himself, even when it meant the loss of a commission or personal advancement.

According to Costa and Rodrigo Mello Franco de Andrade, the final design, developed on site in New York (fig. 28), differed completely from the individual projects previously submitted by each architect but never published.[5] Costa was here open to an even more substantial contribution from the younger architect than he had been in the ministry project. The pavilion's lightness, elegant gracefulness, flowing plastic volume, fluid curves, and water are trademarks of Niemeyer's emerging style. Costa's influence is nonetheless clearly evident in the pavilion's fixed brise-soleil, a perforated concrete

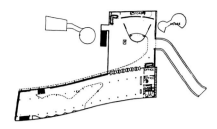

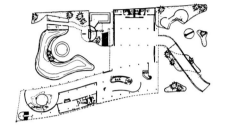

29. Lúcio Costa and Niemeyer,
**Brazilian Pavilion for New York World's
Fair,** 1939, first and second floor plans

screen that recalls the wooden lathe structures of colonial architecture. Costa used such screens later in his Parque Guinle apartments in Rio (1948–54).[6]

The free plan and fluidity of the Brazilian Pavilion answered not only to the commission requirements but also to the conditions of the site, and in particular to the imposing presence of the adjacent monumental French Pavilion (fig. 27). It is both ironic and appropriate that the first independent expression of Brazilian modernism emerged from a desire not to be overshadowed by the contribution of the French, who had dominated Brazilian art throughout the nineteenth century. The Brazilian qualities of flexibility, plasticity, and accommodation expressed in the pavilion thus reflect the long colonial experience of European imperial domination and the Brazilian adaptation to this condition. The pavilion's grace, malleability, and modest elegance reveal the architects' accommodation of the massive French Pavilion.

To minimize the inevitable comparison between the two, Costa and Niemeyer sited their pavilion as far as possible from the French building, and in so doing made creative use of the curved extremity of the corner of the site; they also refused to compete with France's greater resources, choosing instead to emphasize lightness, airy grace, and formal simplicity to contrast with the bulkier French work. They sought a modest yet attractive building that knew its place and held its own through a subtle yet dynamic equilibrium of contrasting properties and graceful formal counterpoints. The building was thus born of formal contrast and cultural differentiation.

Formal contrasts appear on several levels: in the compositional inversion of the curve of the entrance ramp in the exhibition hall wing and of solid and void on the main facade, which shifts from perforated solid on the left to void at the center, to glazed wall on the right. These skillful inversions of solid and void, in and out, and up and down anticipate Niemeyer's next major building, the casino at Pampulha.

Perhaps the most compelling inversion for the visitor was the experience of entering the building via a ramp that led not in but out, to an open-air terrace (the "esplanade") that commanded a splendid view of the curving exhibition wing and the centerpiece below, the tropical pond and garden. The pavilion represented the first Brazilian development of the *promenade architecturale*. The open, fluid plan (fig. 29) invited the visitor to move freely through the exhibition spaces and to enjoy the shifting visual perspectives that always seemed to lead back to the ever-visible garden. From the upper-level terrace, one reached the garden via a small staircase. One could also pause for an audiovisual presentation in the

30. Lúcio Costa and Niemeyer,
**Brazilian Pavilion for New York World's
Fair,** 1939, exhibition gallery

auditorium, buy souvenirs in the gift shop, and then proceed to the gently curving exhibition hall, which was surmounted by a third-level balcony offering additional exhibition space (fig. 30). Entering the building at the ground level, one came first to a tropical birdhouse to the right of the ramp, then to an exhibition gallery that opened onto the garden and pond. In the curved wing to the left of the garden was an information booth, a coffee bar and exhibit, a restaurant and kitchen, and a dance floor and orchestra pit. A curving stairway in the corner of the wing led to the upper exhibition space. The displays were selected and arranged by the German-born architect Paul Lester Wiener, in consultation with government authorities.

The Brazilian Pavilion was more than a momentous achievement in modern architecture. The building effectively projected to the developed world an attractive and compelling image of Brazilian culture as a synthesis of the modern and the exotic. Its free-flowing spaces, dramatic structure, and careful displays reinforced the image of the country as an exotic destination for tourists and a progressive nation that commanded the infrastructure to support them. The pavilion's positive critical reception showed that architecture could be a powerful tool of foreign public relations for a developing country that sought to stimulate tourism and increase its viability as a modern nation-state.

The Pampulha Complex and the Suburban Utopia Niemeyer's work on the Ministry of Education and Health Building put him in contact with powerful government officials, among them Governor Benedito Valladares of Minas Gerais. The governor's interest in developing tourism in his state led him to invite Costa to submit a proposal for a new hotel in Ouro Prêto, the colonial capital of Minas (and also site of much baroque church architecture by Aleijadinho [figs. 4, 5]). The commission required that the new building respect the colonial townscape while providing modern tourist amenities. Costa again stepped aside for Niemeyer, whose picturesque solution for the Grand Hotel was unfortunately compromised by the steep, hillside site and insufficient attention to functional considerations. Niemeyer's building was criticized for its cramped quarters and restrictive planning.[7]

Yet the hotel in Ouro Prêto opened the door to more important commissions from Valladares, whose ambitions for developing leisure infrastructure in Minas included a hilltop casino overlooking the capital city of Belo Horizonte. Perhaps the Ouro Prêto hotel project had made clear the planning difficulties and spatial limitations of mountainside sites; this time Niemeyer took up the governor's

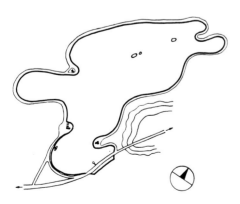

31. **Pampulha,** Minas Gerais, plan showing buildings proposed by Niemeyer around the lake, 1940

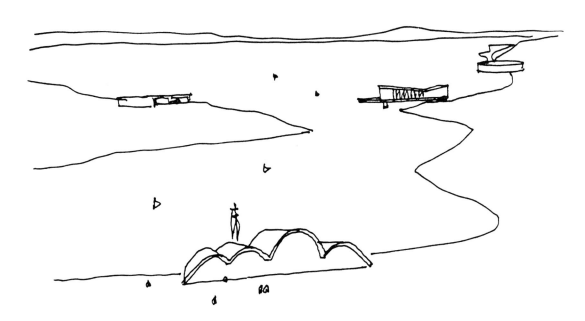

32. Niemeyer,
sketch of proposed buildings on Pampulha
Lake, Minas Gerais, 1940

idea but proposed a location where he could design more freely and expansively, beside an artificial lake in the suburb of Pampulha, fifteen kilometers from Belo Horizonte. Here, against the placid water and the curving contours of the reservoir, the architect proposed a casino building that he envisioned as the nucleus of an entire leisure and entertainment complex for the nouveaux riches of the industrial city (fig. 31). Enthused by the prospect, Juscelino Kubitschek, Belo Horizonte's dynamic mayor decided to carry out the scheme immediately. Thus began the most important working relationship of Niemeyer's career. Kubitschek's patronage at Pampulha and later in Brasília, as president of the Republic, gave rise to Niemeyer's best work and brought further international attention to both architect and Brazilian modernism.

Kubitschek saw the project as an opportunity to create a suburban playground for the local industrial elite, who sought modern leisure facilities in which to reap the fruits of their labors. As we have seen, Brazilian modernization also involved a search for a new cultural identity that would mirror urban progress through innovative form, proving that Brazil was abreast of the latest European developments. As part of a feasibility study for the city's modernization, Kubitschek had previously invited the French beaux-arts urbanist Alfred Agache to study the Pampulha area and propose an urban scheme. Agache was impressed with the monumental classical planning of downtown Belo but shocked by the underdevelopment of the outlying districts. He proposed that Pampulha be developed into a satellite city to

33. Niemeyer,
Casino at Pampulha, Minas Gerais, 1942,
main facade at night

34. Niemeyer,
Casino at Pampulha, Minas Gerais, 1942,
main facade with bronze sculpture (by Zamoiski)

house the city's working classes. Kubitschek, mindful of the need for political backing from the industrial bourgeois, rejected this proposal in favor of his (and their) dream of an elite suburban neighborhood surrounding the lake. Modernity at Pampulha was to consist of an artificial utopia, a center of pleasure and diversion for the upper classes. Privileged members of government, industry, and finance bought up cheap lots, boosting real estate values and private development.[8] Niemeyer was to create the forms.

Pampulha was not conceived as a unified urban ensemble but rather as a series of isolated buildings in nature, each of independent interest. The only unifying element was the lake itself. Five buildings were planned: a gambling casino, a yacht club, a popular dance hall, a church, and a tourist hotel. Only the first four were realized (fig. 32). The mayor subsequently added a second home for himself to set an example for the area's development as a weekend retreat and high-society enclave. With the exception of the church, all of the designs reflect the indulgent spirit of the baroque pleasure pavilion or the modern-day luxury resort. This was a new direction for modern architecture, which had been preoccupied with moral programs, but the shift was in complete agreement with the Latin joie de vivre and the mid-twentieth-century attitudes and aspirations of Brazilian society.

While Niemeyer used the complex to give free reign to his plastic imagination, the ambitious mayor saw it as a vehicle for personal prestige and electoral consolidation among the haute-bourgeois constituency. Typical of the demagogic politics in force since the Vargas revolution of 1930, but reflective as well of paternalist Brazilian society, the project also gestured to the working classes with the proposal for a "popular" dance hall. The scheme bowed as well to traditional Catholic Brazilian society by including a church where one might seem, at first, totally out of place. Excessive drinking and gambling, of course, suggested the need for confession. Niemeyer himself was not repentant: his first major act of iconoclasm, the church of São Francisco de Assis in Pampulha, contained no confessional; it protested all taboos.

The Casino at Pampulha The centerpiece of the Pampulha complex is the casino, erected in 1942 on a scenic promontory overlooking the lake (figs. 33, 34). Visually very prominent to those approaching from the city, it is also clearly visible from the dance hall and yacht club across the lake. Niemeyer seems to have designed the building with a view to the nightly arrival of Belo's polished urbanites. The bright lights of the building's double-height foyer promise evenings of excitement and adventure.

35. Niemeyer,
Casino at Pampulha, Minas Gerais, 1942, section

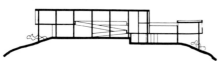

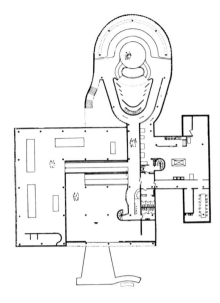

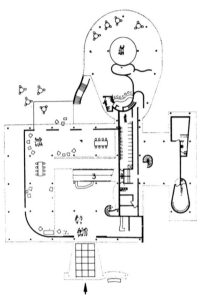

36. Niemeyer,
Casino at Pampulha, Minas Gerais, 1942,
ground and second floor plans

The casino shows Niemeyer's skillful manipulation of International Style elements and Corbusian ideas in the new Brazilian context of elitist modernization. The play of formal contrasts derives from the Brazilian Pavilion, which the casino resembles in a number of ways. Both have orthogonal facades elevated on tall, thin pilotis, and both invite the visitor to experience the building, via ramps and subtly interconnected volumes, as a fluid *promenade architecturale* that encompasses not only interior space but also the changing views of the landscape outside. The garden and pond at the center of the Brazilian Pavilion here lies in front of the building. The main facades of both buildings contrast a wall panel (solid or pseudo-solid) on the left with a glazed void on the right. In the Brazilian Pavilion, the left-hand panel was perforated with a brise-soleil, whereas the casino's corresponding panel is a solid wall with marble revetment. The change accentuates the opposition of solid and void, support and supported. The casino's structural dynamism is especially evident at night, when one observes the contrast between dark masses raised on thin pilotis and brightly lit volumes within. The heavy concrete slab of the entrance canopy, which takes the place of the curving entrance ramp of the Brazilian Pavilion, seems suspended in thin air, as if by magic. Such formal and structural games are completely at home in a building of this type, for they invoke a gambling spirit and present the space and structure of the building itself as an elaborate and entertaining game that the architect is playing, as if to say, "Look at what I can do! Anything can happen here!" The patron is invited to assume a similar mood of adventurous derring-do and confident self-indulgence. The building's rich decor adds to the dazzling effect: a profusion of mirrored walls, pink glass, and chromium-plated columns contrasts with the satin wall hangings and brightly colored *azulejo* wall panels.

The program included, in three distinct but interconnected volumes, gaming rooms, lounges, a bar and restaurant with a stage and floor-lit dance area, a lobby, terraces, dressing rooms, and service facilities (figs. 35, 36). The L-shaped plan of the gaming room, accessible from the ground-floor lobby via a ramp, recalls that of the Brazilian Pavilion exhibition hall, with one important difference: the gaming room has no curved contour. Niemeyer saved his major formal inversion here for the pear-shaped restaurant and dance hall: a dynamic, elliptical free-form element in an otherwise rigidly orthogonal

37 (overleaf). Niemeyer,
Casa do Baile at Pampulha, Minas Gerais,
1942

38. Niemeyer,
Casa do Baile at Pampulha, Minas Gerais,
1942, canopy and azulejo revetments

39. Niemeyer,
Casa do Baile at Pampulha, Minas Gerais, 1942

40. Niemeyer,
Yacht Club at Pampulha, Minas Gerais, 1942

composition. The abrupt transition from the curving dance wing to the main gaming pavilion is smoothed by the gently undulating stair hall that connects the two via a ground-floor terrace on the south side. The casino's planning illustrates even more clearly than the Berço's Niemeyer's ability to unify a complex program with multiple spaces and functions.

Theatrical and hedonistic in treatment, the interior ramps and labyrinthine passages between volumes not only establish the building's circulation routes, but reinforce the social differentiation of the casino's various actors—clients, entertainers, and serving staff—and thus reveal the complex rituals of Brazilian society, as Kenneth Frampton has observed.[9] An ingenious backstage access to the dance hall via an elliptical double corridor allowed waiters and gamblers to enter the restaurant without coming into contact with one another. Niemeyer reinforced the Brazilian dichotomy of served and servant through a spatial funnel that functions as class divider.

The Yacht Club and the Kubitschek House at Pampulha The casino simultaneously fuses and individualizes dynamically juxtaposed volumes, achieving formal unity without sacrificing spatial variety. This characteristic appears in simplified form in the Yacht Club (figs. 40, 41) and Kubitschek House (fig. 42), both of which harness dynamically oblique lines into a convincing geometric clarity and formal purity almost classical in spirit. The source of both buildings is Le Corbusier's 1930 project for the Errazuriz House in Chile. All three foster a felicitous correspondence among practical, functional, and aesthetic considerations, harmonized by reference to simple geometric shapes in perfect balance: two trapezoids meet along their shortest sides, forming the dividing wall between the living and dining areas. This punctured wall guarantees continuity as well as spatial autonomy while corresponding to the single gutter line created by the intersection of the two segments of the reverse-slope roof. The inverted pitch derives ultimately from colonial practice, as do the *azulejo* revetments and the vertical *quebra sol* by now de rigueur in Niemeyer's designs. The yacht club is also an example of *architecture parlant* (speaking architecture): projecting out into the lake, its sleek, streamlined contour and prowlike front recall the elegant yachts that were to sail around it.

The Casa do Baile at Pampulha Niemeyer's design for the Casa do Baile (the popular dance hall and restaurant [figs 37–39]), while indebted to the Corbusian *mariage de contour*, is more his own in form and spirit than either the casino or the yacht club. Echoing the swaying movements of the samba that was to be danced there, its form perfectly fits its function. Whereas in the first two Pampulha buildings the curve is skillfully used only as a counterpoint, in the Casa do Baile, situated on a small island near the edge of the lake, it is the dominant motif. With the exception of columns and window frames, straight lines are entirely absent. The basis of the composition is a meandering canopy of reinforced concrete that connects the two small buildings, a free form that follows the contours of the small island on which it is placed. The canopy, which gives the work its capricious lightness and absolute transparency, became an important theme in Niemeyer's later work, reappearing in the unexecuted project for a hotel for Pampulha, the Ibirapuera Park in São Paulo, and the house at Canoas.

Scenography is paramount in the Casa do Baile. The canopy not only provides protection from rain and sun but frames the view of the lake and the casino on the other side. As Yves Bruand has noted, the canopy paradoxically gives value to the void that it molds. The place, long abandoned but now used as a restaurant, retains the charm that Niemeyer's imagination gave to it. The attention to the natural landscape, the sensitive scale and proportion, and the unity and continuity provided by the circular plan of the dance hall, which takes up the curving theme of the canopy in its exterior, all contribute to this successful design.[10]

The Casa do Baile was surrounded by a tropical garden and lily pond by Roberto Burle Marx, who also designed Portuguese mosaic walkways similar to his pavements for Copacabana beach. Burle Marx also designed the gardens around the casino and the chapel of São Francisco de Assis, Niemeyer's greatest contribution to Pampulha.

The Chapel of São Francisco de Assis at Pampulha The small chapel (figs. 43, 48) is the masterpiece of the Pampulha complex. Here Niemeyer inverted the structures and themes explored in the other buildings in the ensemble, all of which partook of International Style construction deriving from Le Corbusier's Dom-ino House to wish away walls and emphasize spatial interpenetration playfully, in a manner entirely appropriate to programs devoted to worldly pleasures. Niemeyer treated the chapel's serious moral program, however, in a more neo-baroque fashion, focusing on the unity of space and structure, of plan, vision, and religious experience. The shell of the building is a self-supporting parabolic vault that recalls the arches used by Eugene Freyssinet in his airship hangar at Orly (illustrated in Le Corbusier's *Vers une architecture*) and the dynamic structures of Swiss engineer Robert Maillart. This form, used previously only in utilitarian engineering projects, had several advantages for the church program. The vault lent itself

41. Niemeyer,
Yacht Club at Pampulha, Minas Gerais, 1942

42. Niemeyer,
Kubitschek House at Pampulha,
Minas Gerais, 1943

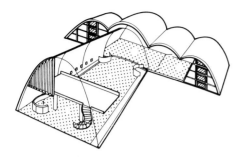

43. Niemeyer,
Chapel of São Francisco de Assis at Pampulha,
Minas Gerais, 1943, axonometric

well to the basilica layout while unifying space and structure by integrating walls and ceiling in one continuous form. As important for Niemeyer, the vault evoked the sculptural lyricism of the Brazilian baroque.

The building is also a masterpiece of scenographic planning, on both exterior and interior. Leaving the Casa do Baile and following the natural *promenade architecturale* around the lake, the pilgrim catches changing views of the building through different natural frames (fig. 47). The structure's true front, the lakeside facade, is meant to be seen from afar and in relation to the pristine nature surrounding it. Approaching from the street, one encounters a brilliant blue and white *azulejo* composition by Candido Portinari depicting scenes from the life of Saint Francis (figs. 46, 49). From the lakefront entrance, one notices how Niemeyer manipulated the parabolic vault to direct the worshipper's attention to the focus at the high altar: Portinari's mural of Saint Francis (fig. 45). The nave narrows and declines as one approaches the altar and sacristy, where the space suddenly widens via an almost imperceptible expansion of the vault in the opposite direction. This visual surprise is accentuated by the skillful play of light and by the counterpoint established between the nave, with its dark wood revetment, and the choir, which is brightly and mysteriously lit by an invisible source (fig. 50). The rays of light, concentrated on Portinari's vast mural (which occupies the entire rear wall), come from the lantern at the intersection of the two parabolic vaults, invisible to the viewer since the choir vault section is slightly wider than that of the nave here.

The building exhibits a harmonious blend of asymmetrical dynamism and compositional balance and of curved, straight, and oblique lines arranged in a vital point and counterpoint. The graceful curves of the helical staircase, the pulpit, and the baptistry font contrast with the heavy horizontal slab of the gallery, which seems to float miraculously above the nave. On the exterior, the vertical lines of the brise-soleil panels provide a counterpoint to the curving contour of the vault and the floating slab of the slightly inclined entrance canopy. This slab in turn prepares one for the structural magic of the gallery within and counterpoints the oblique vertical lines of the freestanding, hollow bell tower to the right of the entrance. While the chapel's composition expresses plastic unity and spatial continuity, it also clearly distinguishes the constituent volumes—nave, choir, and sacristy—and the structural components of the vaults and walls, which function as decorative screens with glazing (on the front) and *azulejos* and murals (on the rear). The dynamic

44. Niemeyer,
Chapel of São Francisco de Assis at Pampulha,
Minas Gerais, 1943, main entrance

equilibrium thus established results in a plastic freedom and structural lightness at the heart of Niemeyer's best work.

The works at Pampulha, especially the Casa do Baile and the chapel, illustrate Niemeyer's first major attempts to push reinforced concrete to its sculptural limits. Le Corbusier once said to Niemeyer, oversimplifying matters somewhat, "You do Baroque in reinforced concrete, but you do it very well."[11] Niemeyer and many critics see Pampulha as the true beginning of modern Brazilian architecture. Here Niemeyer freed modern architecture of the rigid prescriptions of orthogonal design by demonstrating the plastic and expressive potentials of reinforced concrete and by achieving lyrical structural lightness, sculptural freedom, and curved monumentality. Yet as Bruand has pointed out, the chapel was less of a real break with the past than an overcoming of rigid principles, a challenge to established theories, and an affirmation of the artist's right to almost unlimited formal imagination. The design is also logical in its exploration of the ultimate nature of modern material, valuing its ductility and sculptural potential.[12]

Niemeyer wrote that his free-form architecture at Pampulha arose to protest "rational architecture," the rectilinear, mechanized forms of the European International Style: "Everything started when I began the Pampulha studies—my first phase—deliberately despising the exalted right angle and the rationalist architecture made by ruler and square. . . . I protested against this monotonous and repetitive architecture, so easy to elaborate that in a short time it spread quickly from the United States to Japan." Speaking of the sources of the varied curves and unexpected boldness of the Pampulha church, the architect wrote: "The intended protest arose from the environment where I lived, with its white beaches, its huge mountains, its old baroque churches, and its beautiful tanned women. I had within me not only Rio's mountains, as Le Corbusier once observed, but everything that touched me emotionally."[13] These four elements—white beaches, huge mountains, old baroque churches, and beautiful tanned women—these architectures native to Brazil touched Niemeyer most deeply and formed the stuff of his dreams and his best creations. Common to all are the sensual and free-flowing curve, the basis of his aesthetic and Brazil's tropical civilization and a theme that he would explore more deeply in the house at Canoas.

As for Niemeyer's political sentiments about the Pampulha program, it is important to note that his involvement in the project preceded his official association with the Brazilian Communist

45. Niemeyer, **Chapel of São Francisco de Assis** at Pampulha, Minas Gerais, 1943, mural in high altar (by Candido Portinari) showing scenes from the life of St. Francis

46 (overleaf). Niemeyer, **Chapel of São Francisco de Assis** at Pampulha, Minas Gerais, 1943, azulejo mural (designed by Candido Portinari)

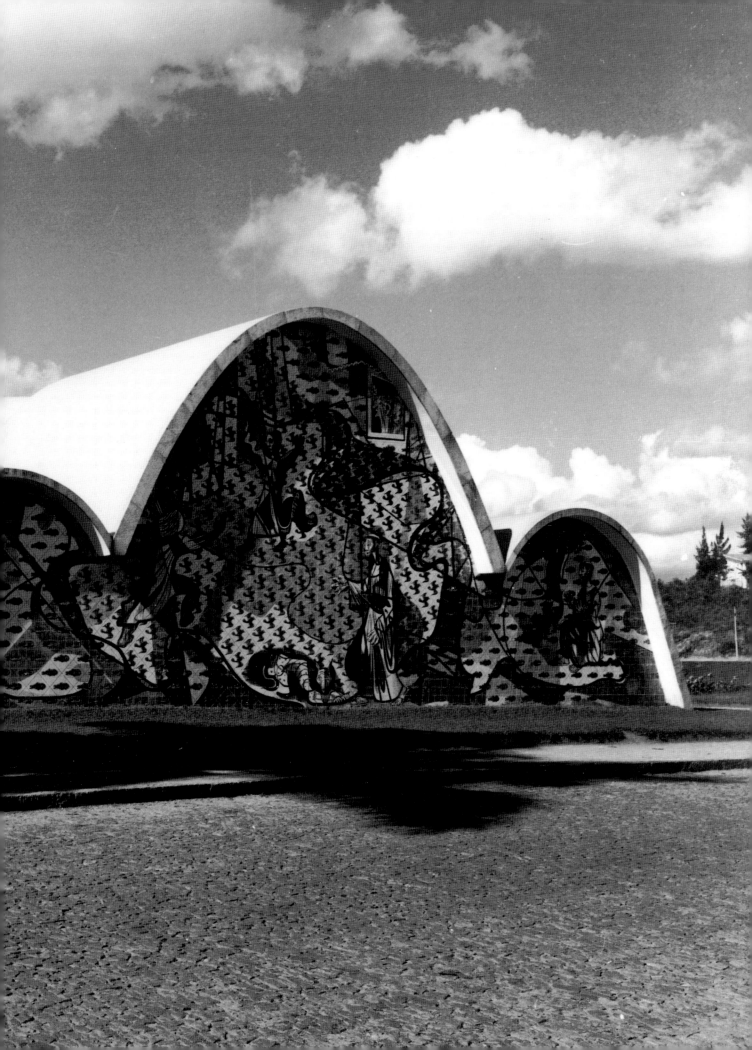

47. Niemeyer,
Chapel of São Francisco de Assis at Pampulha,
Minas Gerais, 1943, distant view from lake

party, of which he declared himself a member in 1945. As did Le Corbusier, Niemeyer cautiously separated architecture and politics, especially when an important commission was at stake. Despite his basic conviction that the architect should be involved in solving collective problems through grand projects of "social architecture," Niemeyer has never hesitated to develop sumptuous schemes for elite patrons. He later justified his position by arguing that a purely social architecture (especially of the Bauhaus-derived workers' housing type) would impoverish Brazil's architecture by denying what was new, creative, and Brazilian about it. As early as 1955 he saw forcing Brazilians into European working-class cubes as a betrayal of a national artistic objective. For him, architecture was first and foremost a plastic art that should faithfully express what was imposed by the environment—broadly conceived. Thus, Brazil's architecture should reflect both the contours and conditions of a given site and the technical, political, and economic limitations of its society. In an underdeveloped nation with a powerful elite and little industrial infrastructure, broad-based social architecture was not possible. Niemeyer felt that a truly Brazilian architecture must reject the hard-edged, cold architecture of

48. Niemeyer,
Chapel of São Francisco de Assis at Pampulha,
Minas Gerais, 1943, lake facade

the "European tendency" in favor of a more lyrical, curving, and plastic art that often seems less concerned with social function than with formal innovation based on structural experimentation and the plastic potential of reinforced concrete.[14]

The Pampulha Complex: Conclusion and Aftermath Kubitschek's utopian project was plagued with problems from the start. Left to private speculation, the area failed to develop according to any overall master plan that would have guaranteed infrastructural viability. Housing, which would have fostered long-term consumption of the project's services, was not built. Other unforeseeable problems arose: President Eurico Gaspar Dutra's 1946 prohibition of gambling, the discovery of parasites in the lake, and the breaking of the dam and resulting fall in the water level. Niemeyer's designs, for all their formal beauty and charm, were betrayed by circumstances and remained isolated, pristine, and devoid of their intended functions. The casino was transformed into an art museum; the dance hall never functioned, except as a restaurant. Only the yacht club served as intended, though its use was severely limited by the problems with the lake. The church too met with problems: its unprecedented form created a scandal among local parishioners who could not understand it, and the local archbishop refused to consecrate it because of its revolutionary qualities. It has been only occasionally used for special services and was at one point transformed into a radio station. The fate of Pampulha reinforced the severe criticism of European commentators like Max Bill who, insensitive to any values other than those of social function, condemned Niemeyer's innovations as gratuitous and arbitrary formalism.[15]

The more recent history of Pampulha illustrates the further betrayal of the original dream. In 1987 one observer, a local journalist, noted that the "picture post card was dying": "The tourist who sees the luxurious mansions in the vicinity is not aware of the nearby *favelas* (shantytowns) and the illegal housing lots with no sanitation infrastructure that cause pollution run-off into the tributaries that feed the lake." When created in 1936, the reservoir was supposed to supply the capital with water for fifty years, but by 1987 an estimated 15 percent of the basin had become polluted with four million cubic meters of solid waste. The lake had become a huge sewage receptacle that would take years and millions of dollars to clean up. According to urbanist Radames Teixeira, the only thing Brazilians could do was to watch it expire like a loved one dying from an incurable illness.

49. Niemeyer,
Chapel of São Francisco de Assis at Pampulha,
Minas Gerais, 1943, facade with azulejo design
(by Candido Portinari)

In 1988, however, a $250-million cleanup and rehabilitation project was proposed, to be funded by a combination of private investment, an improvement tax to be levied on local residents, and World Bank funds. The ambitious project included constructing islands, an ecological and aquatic park, restaurants, an international hotel and convention center, a shopping mall, more leisure facilities, and a monument to honor Juscelino Kubitschek floating on the lake (proposed by Niemeyer). The municipal authorities promised to build all of this in a record twenty-four months. The rehabilitation proposal was highly polemical since local residents, who were to be forced to contribute financially to the project, were left out of the decision-making process. A more basic problem has been the lack of political commitment to real improvement: new sewage systems, unlike Niemeyer's proposed monument to the glory of Kubitschek, are not visible works that bring political prestige to those who carry them out. [16]

Projects Between the Pampulha Complex and the Canoas House Pampulha was the focus of Niemeyer's development of new structures and volumetric forms made possible by his exploration of the plastic potential of reinforced concrete. For the next ten years Niemeyer continued this investigation, taking Pampulha and the work of Le Corbusier as his point of departure. Focusing on pilotis and vaults, he went well beyond Le Corbusier in striving for more vigorous and exuberant plastic inventions based on these elements. Niemeyer's arch and vault structures reached their zenith around 1950; the new piloti experiments began the following year. Niemeyer was interested in arches and vaults as a means to unify structures with his preferred curves. The low vault projected for the unexecuted Oswaldo de Andrade House (1938), for instance, recalls Le Corbusier's 1935 weekend house in a Paris suburb. [17] The huge arch of the (unexecuted) stadium for Rio (1941), with cables supporting part of the roof, derives from Le Corbusier's Palace of the Soviets (1931) and project for the University of Brazil (1936). But Pampulha proved that Niemeyer had evolved a unique personal language, and from 1943 to 1951 he varied and refined previously elaborated themes and forms: the parabolic vaults of Pampulha reappear in the nautical club on the Lagoa Rodrigo de Freitas (1944), the Tremaine House in California (1947), the theater project for the Ministry of Education and Health Building (1948), the Duchen Factory near São Paulo (with Helio Uchoa, 1950), the Clube de Quinhentos in Guaratinguetá (1951), and the Youth Club in Diamantina (1950). The dynamic structures of the latter suggest the influence of

50 Niemeyer,
Chapel of São Francisco de Assis at Pampulha, Minas Gerais, 1943, interior looking toward choir

Robert Maillart, the Swiss specialist in bridges and reinforced concrete construction.[18]

The Diamantina project relates to the projected annex for Niemeyer's Hospital Sul-América (1952; figs. 53, 54), in which arches contrast with a rectilinear main block and allude to the natural background formed by the peak of Corcovado Mountain. The project reveals his evolution of the piloti form and his desire to increase the building's lightness and structural freedom. Le Corbusier had initiated the separation of the piloti from the mass that it supported in the Swiss Pavilion at the University City in Paris (1930–32) and had pushed this distinction even farther in the Unité d'Habitation in Marseilles, where paired pilotis tilt open toward the top; this and their brutalist treatment make them active plastic elements in the design, and not mere structural components. Niemeyer was more concerned with the transitions between the supports and the block: he wanted to maximize the space available on the ground and not visually overload the design with unnecessary structural elements that would make the building look heavy. To achieve these goals he developed V-shaped and W-shaped pilotis that channeled the vertical thrusts of the two or three structural columns in the levels above to the ground.

The hospital's V-shaped piloti (fig. 51) is an ingenious solution, both aesthetically and practically, because it eliminates the multiplicity of pillars and columns and the impression of a forest of columns in three or four parallel rows. The building appears lighter, the structural elements more expressive. The dynamic effect results from the proportions of the pilotis and their contrast with the static rectangular block above. That they are thinner as they approach the mass being supported reinforces the impression of lightness. The hospital also sets up an opposition of color and texture: the white of the concrete versus the red of the hollow panels of the brise-soleils, which recall those on the facades of Costa's Parque Guinle buildings, especially Nova Cintra and Bristol.

The tall, thin V-shaped pilotis first emerged in the 1950 project for a large apartment complex (the Quitandinha Apartment-Hotel) in Petrópolis, but that building's scale overwhelmed the effect. They took complete form the following year in the Palace of Agriculture, part of a vast complex of interconnected pavilions projected for São Paulo's Ibirapuera Park in 1954 for the Fourth Centennial Exhibition (to commemorate the founding of the city), and in the building designed for the Hansa Quarter in Berlin (1955; fig. 52). Niemeyer's W-shaped pilotis are less successful because they look cumbersome; they appear in the Conjunto Residencial Governador Kubitschek in Belo Horizonte (1951) and in the California Building in São Paulo (1951–54).[19]

Max Bill vehemently criticized Niemeyer's piloti experiments as examples of a

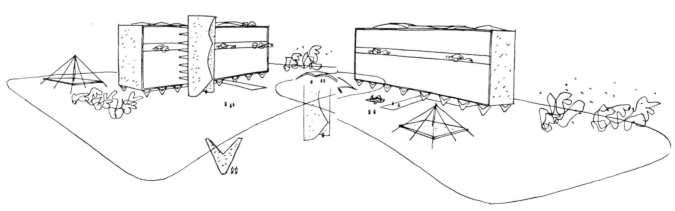

51. Niemeyer,
Hospital Sul-América, Rio de Janeiro, 1952,
pilotis

52. Niemeyer,
sketches for proposed apartment complex
in the Hansa Quarter, Berlin, 1955

53, 54. Niemeyer,
project for Hospital Sul-América,
Rio de Janeiro, 1952, model in photomontage with
annex to left (above) and third–sixth floor plan (right)

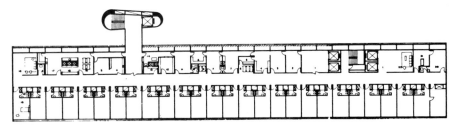

55. Niemeyer,
State High School auditorium,
Belo Horizonte, Minas Gerais, 1954

56, 57. Niemeyer,
State High School auditorium,
Belo Horizonte, Minas Gerais, 1954, model and
building under construction

58. Niemeyer,
Julia Kubitschek Elementary School,
Diamantina, Minas Gerais, 1951

decadent and irresponsible formalism. Speaking of the Palace of Industry in the Ibira-puera Park in São Paulo, another element in the fourth centennial celebration building plan, he observed:

In a street here in São Paulo I have seen under construction a building in which pilotis construction is carried to extremes one would have supposed impossible. There I saw some shocking things, modern architecture sunk to the depths, a riot of anti-social waste, lacking any sense of responsibility toward either the business occupant or his customers. . . . Thick pilotis, thin pilotis, pilotis of whimsical shapes lacking any struc-tural rhyme or reason, disposed all over the place. . . . One is baffled to account for such barbarism as this in a country where there is a CIAM group, a country in which international congresses on modern architecture are held, where a journal like Habitat is published and where there is a biennial exhibition of architecture. For such works are born of a spirit devoid of all decency and of all responsibility to human needs. It is the spirit of decorativeness, something diametrically opposed to the spirit which animates architecture, which is the art of building, the social art above all others.[20]

Pure Volume, Dynamic Structure, and the Evolution of Free Form Niemeyer, having evolved the V-shaped piloti and separated it from the slab it supported, took the next step: a more daring and disciplined integration of this new structural form with the pure volume of the building itself. Two 1951 works in Diamantina, a school and a hotel (figs. 58, 59), synthesize form, structure, and volume by wedding the pilotis to the essential volume of the building. (Along with the club, these projects were commissioned by Kubitschek to bring progress to his hometown). Typical is Niemeyer's inverted trapezoid, a form first explored in the inclined facade of the unexecuted first project for the Kubitschek House in Pampulha and later taken up in the house for Mrs. Prudente de Morais in Rio (1949) and in the row houses for the Centro Técnico da Aeronáutica de São José dos Campos, one hundred kilometers from São Paulo (1947–53).

In the two buildings in Diamantina, the architect turned a prism on its head and raised it on pilotis, now dynamically integrated with the building's volume, to achieve an entirely new effect. Niemeyer's solution clearly suggests the

59. Niemeyer,
Tijuca Hotel, Diamantina, Minas Gerais, 1951

60. Niemeyer,
apartment building on the Praça da Liberdade,
Belo Horizonte, 1954–55

desire to protect the bedrooms of the hotel and classrooms of the school from excessive sunlight by projecting the roof slab outward, but its elaboration reflects his concern for developing a simple, elegant, and original volume. The hotel, unlike that of Ouro Prêto, is well planned so that the elements on the facade are carefully unified. The upward and outward slope seems to derive naturally from the transversal V-shaped pilotis, one arm of which supports only the slab of the first floor, while the other extends to the roof slab and fuses skillfully with the walls that separate the terraces and apartments behind. In the school (named for Kubitschek's mother), the classic pilotis of the ground level and the diagonal braces that support the roof slab on the upper level are completely distinct and independent from one another, emphasizing the autonomy of the main story and its relative detachment from the ground. In both works, structural, formal, and volumetric elements fuse harmoniously. Both occupy important places in Niemeyer's work because they represent successful attempts to integrate an entire program in a single volume that is both pure and original. The two buildings inspired Affonso Reidy's similar structural investigations in the Colégio Paraguai-Brasil in Assuncíon (1953–65) and the Museu de Arte Moderna in Rio (1954–67).

Niemeyer's structural experiments in the early fifties all create new forms via the flexibility of concrete, but he also explored sculptural forms independent of strictly structural considerations. His most characteristic achievement, his synthesis of curvilinear form with free and novel structure, appears in the 1954 auditorium of the State High School in Belo Horizonte (figs. 55–57). The design contrasts the curving structure of the auditorium and the simple rectangular volumes of the principle block containing the classrooms, but here the contrast is at the expense of equilibrium. Niemeyer inverted the logical hierarchy of several of his works of this period. The auditorium, secondary in function to the school, becomes the primary focus of aesthetic exploration: the functional periphery becomes the aesthetic center. The building's shape is not, however, a function of arbitrary formal innovation. The eye-shaped auditorium speaks of the problems of visibility addressed by the design and indeed of the very function of an auditorium.

In addition to exploring the plastic potential of reinforced concrete to free the slab from its piloti structure and evolving a new plastic vocabulary of independent structures such as that at the State High School, Niemeyer also sought to free the slab itself from its rectangular form. Curving contours first appear in apartment slabs in the project for the Quitandinha Hotel in Petrópolis (1950) and the Copan Building in São Paulo (1951–57). Only the latter was carried out (fig. 64). The Copan Build-

61. Niemeyer,
Fourth Centennial Exposition of São Paulo,
Ibirapuera Park, São Paulo, 1954, model

ing, Niemeyer's Brazilian answer to the Corbusian *unité d'habitation,* uses an S-shaped plan echoing, in a disciplined and regularized way, the contours of Le Corbusier's curving ribbon of apartment slabs in the Rio project of 1929, as do those of the Pedregulho apartment block designed by Reidy at about the same time (1950–52).

The entirely free form is most evident in Niemeyer's great covered walk, or concrete canopy, for Ibirapuera (1951–54; figs. 61, 63); in the Canoas House he designed for himself in Rio (1953–54); and in the apartment building on the Praça da Liberdade in Belo Horizonte (1954–55; fig. 60). The meandering canopy of Ibirapuera, unifying the exposition pavilions, recalls the free forms of Roberto Burle Marx's gardens, the landscape architect with whom Niemeyer had been continually associated. But Ibirapuera, the architect's first effort to create a unified monumental ensemble, is something of a failure—in part because it was not fully executed as planned, in part because the view of the canopy from above is more impressive than the experience of walking beneath it. Yet the architect's concern for dynamism and flexibility can be clearly seen in the play of ramps, which had the major role in the effect of spatial fluidity in the interiors.

The Niemeyer House at Canoas

The house an architect builds for himself may be considered in general a manifestation of his aspirations, a kind of witness, a confession of his sins, a holograph in which one can not only examine the visible text but also graphically trace the secret motives of the text and the deep-running roots of the poet's inspiration.

—Ernesto Rogers, *Architectural Review,* 1954

The ultimate statement of Niemeyer's mature free-form modernism, a manifesto of the movement and perhaps his masterpiece, is the house he designed for himself in 1953 on the Canoas Road near the São Conrado district of Rio de Janeiro (figs. 62, 65–71). The Canoas House occupies a position in Niemeyer's work and thought similar to that of certain other famous modern houses: Frank Lloyd Wright's Fallingwater, Le Corbusier's Villa Savoie, and Philip Johnson's Glass House. All are masterworks of domestic architecture that reflect the central ideals and personal approaches of their respective architects, especially concerning the relationships among architecture, technology, and nature. The significance of the Canoas House in Niemeyer's work and in the history of modern architecture is best understood in this context.

Set on a steep mountain site in the midst of a dense tropical forest overlooking the sea, the house is a small domestic pavilion defined by a free-form roof derived from the meandering canopy of the Casa do Baile at Pampulha. At Canoas, Niemeyer developed the idea of the canopy as a basic shelter open to and in harmony with nature. The thin, horizontal concrete slab roof cut into a series of flowing curves borrowed from the natural context seems to cover an indefinite space that flows beyond it on all sides. Supported by several widely dispersed, thin steel pilotis that enable the walls to be almost entirely glazed, the slab seems to float magically above the shadowy volume of the house. The house's most remarkable features are its almost complete integration with the natural elements of the site and apparent neutralization of the conventional distinction between architecture and nature. Niemeyer stated:

My concern was to design this residence with complete liberty, adapting it to the irregularities of the terrain, without changing it, and making it curved, so as to permit the vegetation to penetrate, without being separated by the straight line. And I created for the living rooms a zone of shade, so that the glazed walls wouldn't need curtains and the house would be transparent as I preferred.[21]

The Canoas House is a masterpiece of modernist inversion that has as its central theme the apparent resolution of paradox. Here Niemeyer abandoned the Corbusian five-points system previously exploited in the Lagoa House. He inverts the modernist convention of elevating the building on pilotis, bringing the house back down to earth in closer communion with the *natural* nature of the moun-

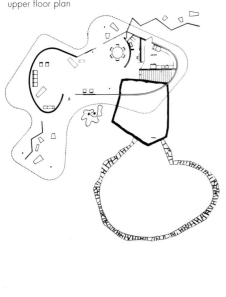

62. Niemeyer,
Canoas House, Rio de Janeiro, 1953–54,
upper floor plan

tain, from which it seems to grow, as does the huge boulder of *carioca* granite that is its centerpiece. The second inversion concerns the functional planning of the house, which appears to be one continuous level, that of the terrace and pool. We do not see the real living quarters, which are below. Niemeyer inverted the conventional domestic arrangement of public space downstairs and private space upstairs by creating a cavelike basement for the bedrooms and bathrooms. The master bedroom offers a dramatic, rectilinear, "framed" view of nature, clearly a parody of the Corbusian approach (fig. 69). In this cozy interior, the resident may effectively hibernate, like a tropical sloth bear, away from the heat or rain or noise of Rio de Janeiro.

The third inversion concerns transportation and access: one must first go up the hill by car before descending into the house on foot. As one goes

63. Niemeyer,
Fourth Centenary Exposition of São Paulo,
Ibirapuera Park, São Paulo, 1954

64. Niemeyer,
Copan Building, São Paulo, 1951–57

inside, one also is aware of the outside. Niemeyer's Brazilian Pavilion also clearly echoes here, for Canoas presents the ultimate development in Brazilian domestic architecture of the *promenade architecturale*. Le Corbusier had mastered this strategy in the Villa Savoie, but the two houses present very different paths. Common to both is a gradual unfolding of truths somewhat at odds with one's first impressions of the buildings. Both approaches assume an automobile; the drive to Niemeyer's house from the beach areas of the *zona sul* is up the long and winding Canoas Road—a sort of elite *subida do morro* (ascent to a *favela*). At the property gate along the serpentine road, one must leave the car and approach the house on foot. In the Villa Savoie, the movement of the car up the driveway and around and then under the house is intended to be an integral part of the experience of getting into the building and divining its purist meaning. In the Canoas House, one must leave modern technology behind and enter an entirely new realm in which the machine metaphor and the deliberately controlled spatial progression (leading up a ramp to carefully framed perspectives of nature) is replaced by a new spatial (and spiritual) experience: that of the free movement of the individual in intimate communion with a timeless nature.

From the entrance gate, a gently curving ramp gradually descends to the grounds, and the house becomes visible—a tropical oasis far from the boisterous crowds of center city and beach. The first impression is of luxuriant color, as the deep greens of the foliage reflect off the still waters of the shallow pool, its contours echoed in the spreading roof slab that hovers, as if by some mysterious force, above the house. At the center of the composition, the huge granite boulder rises up from the earth's crust, echoing in miniature the bare stones of the mountains of the Serra do Mar that tower above the house. The boulder is not just another rock: it symbolizes the timeless geological processes that brought Niemeyer's beloved *carioca* landscapes into existence, the natural parabolas that are the stuff of his architecture, and the spiritual presence that gives this house a sense of transcendence, permanence, and belonging. The boulder anchors the composition visually with its pyramidal mass and earth-gray color, which blends perfectly with that of the roof slab above. The boulder unifies and stabilizes the whole; its mass centers the outward-flowing volumes. It partakes of the water of the pool, the space of the exterior terrace, and the interior volume, without breaking the fluid line of the roof or questioning its magical structural autonomy.

At Canoas Niemeyer created a Brazilian organic architecture that rivals Wright's Fallingwater, which the Brazilian architect most certainly knew. Wright planned the Bear Run house around a symbolic boulder, but whereas Wright's

65. Niemeyer,
Canoas House, Rio de Janeiro, 1953–54,
canopy against mountains

66. Niemeyer,
Canoas House, Rio de Janeiro, 1953–54,
boulder and stairway to lower level

composition is controlled by the rectilinear grid of a modular plan and crisp rectangular cantilevers, the only straight lines at Canoas are the frames of the Corbusian windows and the vertical lines of the cylindrical pilotis. The water at Canoas is not falling but perfectly still. Despite the dynamic curving composition and fluid spaces and volumes, the house is imbued with a classical serenity accentuated by its idyllic, even Olympian setting and by the abstracted classical statues by Alfredo Ceschiatti set about the premises. Niemeyer's Canoas House is a brilliant free-form synthesis of the organic and the classical. This organic classicism goes beyond the Wrightian ideal of organic architecture and the Corbusian notion of the *mariage de contour* to create an architecture that also transcends the classical imitation of nature: the major formal elements of the Canoas House *are* the forms of nature—the sand and water of the concrete slab, the water of the pool, the boulder, and the vegetation.

The Canoas House develops the theme of modernist pavilion architecture by domesticating it, as did Johnson in his Glass House. Both houses have classically serene settings; both are firmly planted on the ground; and both use extensive glazing to open their interiors to the outside. Yet Johnson's classicism is that of the collector—fussy, correct, and archaeological—whereas Niemeyer's is abstract and evocative, more symbiotically at home with the paradoxes of art and nature, classical and modern, nature and technology. Niemeyer deemphasizes the steel frame that Johnson celebrates: Niemeyer handles technology naturally and effortlessly to create a wholly modern and miraculous structural effect. The transparent glass and dark pilotis, obscured in the shadows of the house volume, enable the architect to wish away the elements and materials of modern European technology. The house instead celebrates the plastic freedom of the architect who imaginatively responds to the lyrical forms of Brazil's natural milieu. At Canoas, Niemeyer let nature be his decorator.

The Canoas House synthesizes ideas rooted in Niemeyer's own experiments in the Brazilian Pavilion and Pampulha, where the dynamic visual experience of Brazil's natural milieu of water and tropical foliage dominates. Burle Marx's landscaping at the Canoas House was more than partly responsible for the building's vital integration with its site. His free-form investigations in landscape architecture no doubt had significant impact on Niemeyer.

The poetry of Canoas was misunderstood by the critics, who saw a hopelessly romantic confusion of elements or an arbitrary act of self-indulgence. Walter Gropius, for instance, complained to the architect: "Your house is very beautiful, but it is not multipliable."[22] Obviously Niemeyer was not

67 (overleaf). Niemeyer,
Canoas House, Rio de Janeiro, 1953–54

68. Niemeyer,
Canoas House, Rio de Janeiro, 1953–54,
living room

seeking a standardized solution of the type preferred by the Bauhaus: Canoas was a revolt against that very idea. Nor was Niemeyer seeking a romantic escape into nature and the past. His was a new, thoroughly twentieth-century symbiosis of conflicting categories that the nineteenth-century mind had been unable to reconcile. Canoas is Niemeyer's first great utopian synthesis, a highly personal statement that sought to *neutralize* the basic philosophical distinction between art as something created and artificial and nature as something to be harnessed by technology. The ultimate paradox is that this compelling image of neutralization—the house's near total reconciliation of art and nature—is achieved by subtly manipulating the modern techniques that Niemeyer seeks to deny. Yet the house's "natural" effect remains its most important quality. Italian architect Ernesto Rogers, visiting Brazil on the occasion of the Fourth Centennial Exhibition in São Paulo, vividly recalls his visit to the house with Lúcio Costa:

I doubt that I shall ever forget that scene: the sun was just dipping below the horizon, leaving us in a dark sea of orange, violet, green, and indigo. The house repeated the themes of that orgiastic countryside (incense and the hum of insects); a vast rhapsody beginning in the roof vibrated down the walls and their niches to finish in the pool, where the water, instead of being neatly dammed up, freely spread along the rocks of a kind of forest pool.[23]

Niemeyer's works in the Ibirapuera Park, at Canoas, and on the Praça da Liberdade are exceptional free-form achievements that emerged amid an evolution toward greater formal discipline based on volumetric simplicity. From combining masses, Niemeyer moved to complex interpenetrations of volumes, then to the juxtaposition of independent forms that balance one another in large compositions, and finally to simple, isolated volumes in a vast space. Dynamic formal oppositions based on pure volumes and daring structures would soon be given freer reign in the vast expanse of open space that was to become Brasília. The architecture of Brazil's new capital was a product of Niemeyer's continuing search for formal innovation, a search increasingly classical in inspiration and, paradoxically, ever more surreal in effect.

69. Niemeyer,
Canoas House, Rio de Janeiro, 1953–54,
bedroom window on lower level

70. Niemeyer,
Canoas House, Rio de Janeiro, 1953–54,
view through living room

71 (overleaf). Niemeyer,
Canoas House, Rio de Janeiro, 1953–54,
interior looking toward boulder and dining space

A Classicism for the *Sertão*

Walter Gropius called Niemeyer his "tropical bird of paradise," conjuring up images of a youthful imagination spreading its wings to escape the cage of academic canons and European conventions. The formal innovations of Pampulha and Canoas were indeed the products of a free spirit seeking to liberate itself from the constraints of an imported European system. Yet Niemeyer's most typical work, like that of Le Corbusier, always evokes a powerful tension between liberty and control. Just as Niemeyer was elaborating his free forms during the 1950s, the most fertile period of his career, he was feeling a strong pull back toward a more disciplined architecture. Two events reinforced this tendency, already evident in some of his earlier architecture. The first was the criticism of his work by several European architects who traveled to Brazil for the Fourth Centennial Exhibition in São Paulo (January–February 1954), among them Gropius, Ernesto Rogers, and Max Bill. The second was Niemeyer's 1954 trip to Europe, in which he covered the entire continent from Lisbon to Moscow, with stops in Paris, Venice, Berlin, and elsewhere. Niemeyer responded to these influences by entering a period of critical and retrospective reflection that led to his mature style and theoretical writings. These, however, were less theory than ex post facto attempts to defend his works and explain his ideas to the critics.[1]

Niemeyer's Theory of Architecture Niemeyer's theoretical orientation, latent until 1955, the year that he founded the journal *Módulo*, was rooted in several major points. Underlying his entire oeuvre is the Corbusian conception, reinforced by Lúcio Costa, of architecture as a plastic art and the architect as above all a creator of forms. Niemeyer stressed that the engineer's focus on efficiency, economy, and function is unacceptable for architects because it reduces architecture to a technical formula, resulting in the cold sensibility and standardized banality that he disliked in the work of Gropius and the Bauhaus. Instead, Niemeyer preferred the emotive and poetic side of Le Corbusier, whose definition of architecture as "the skillful, accurate, and magnificent play of masses seen in light" took on a new significance in the sculptural landscapes and radiant sun of tropical Brazil.

Niemeyer's celebration of architecture as visual poetry and his objection to standardization determined the second major aspect of his theory: the replacement of a European functionalist aesthetic with a Brazilian "aesthetic functionalism," according to which "form follows beauty." As Niemeyer wrote in an imaginary Socratic dialogue taking place before the Doge's Palace in Venice: "When a form creates beauty, it becomes functional and thus fundamental in architecture."[2] For Niemeyer, of course, this was no arbitrary formula: beauty depended, as we have seen, on the architect's

72. Niemeyer,
Planalto Palace, Brasília, 1958–60

ability to echo the curving forms of nature, especially the topographic features and female bodies of his native Brazil.

Niemeyer's infatuation with pure and sensual form made him refuse to be shackled by what he saw as the most naive aspect of European modernism: the notion of the architect as social reformer. Niemeyer clearly saw Le Corbusier's charge "architecture or revolution" for the slogan that it was. Niemeyer felt that although the architect should promote a "social architecture" by participating in reform projects when given the chance, the first task is to create expressive forms that distinguish Brazilian achievement from European functionalism. Thus, he argues that imposing on Brazil a social architecture of the type sponsored by the Bauhaus reformers would deny what was most special about Brazilian architecture: its creative vigor and formal innovation. The key to achieving this creative vitality lay in the fourth component of Niemeyer's theory: the reliance on new techniques and materials, in particular reinforced concrete, that freed creative expression. Niemeyer saw reinforced concrete as the material and technical basis for an aesthetic revolution that made possible a new vocabulary of more expressive forms. Concrete was not only the key to Niemeyer's artistic freedom, it was especially appropriate to Brazilian architecture because its inherent malleability echoed the plasticity of the colonial baroque. Moreover, concrete's basic ingredients—sand, stone, and water for the aggregate; clay and limestone for the cement—are both natural and readily available in Brazil. At a time when structural steel was expensive and imported, reinforced concrete construction offered an alternative well suited to a developing nation with a large unskilled labor force. Concrete allowed Niemeyer a broader collaboration among architect, structural engineer, and laborer, the unsung heroes of Brazilian modernism.

Critical Reflection and Formal Evolution Niemeyer fully realized that his travels and critical reflection marked a change in his career, announced in his projects for the Museu de Arte Moderna in Caracas and for Brasília. He started simplifying, concentrating on clear, original, single volumes that derived their expressive effect from visual unity within dramatic landscapes. Such unified forms began to replace compositions based on multiple elements, which had until then typified his style. Niemeyer discussed these changes in a revealing testimony published in *Módulo* in 1958:

The works in progress in Brasília, together with my project for the Caracas Museum, mark a new stage in my professional work, a stage characterized by a constant search for conciseness and purity, and greater attention to the fundamental problems of architecture. This stage, which constitutes a change in my method of design and principally in my way of developing a project, did not arise without reflection. It did not emerge as a new formula answering to new problems; rather, it sprang from a cool and frank review of my work as an architect.[3]

His critical reflection led not only to important changes in his design method but to a basic shift in his professional attitude. Prior to the European trip, Niemeyer had tended to see his work as "an exercise to be undertaken in a sporting spirit—and nothing more." This attitude, resulting in "a certain negligence" reinforced by his "easy-going Bohemian nature," led him to take on too many projects and to rely on his plentiful powers of improvisation to complete them quickly. This approach, he conceded, was responsible for what he and the critics considered the major shortcoming of his early oeuvre: an "excessive tendency toward originality," fed by elite patrons who, unconcerned about larger social issues, sought showy and novel creations that would be discussed in fashionable circles.[4]

Niemeyer's "negligent" approach was rooted less in an irresponsible disposition than in his sober evaluation of the socioeconomic realities of an underdeveloped nation dominated by elite patronage. Skeptical about the possibilities for real reform through architecture under such circumstances, he quickly concluded that "those who dedicated themselves to architecture body and soul must be very naive."[5] But he continued to express guilt-ridden ambivalence about what an architect could and should do. In the 1954 preface to a monograph by Stamo Papadaki presenting Niemeyer's early works, the architect wrote:

Architecture must express the spirit of the technical and social forces that are predominant in a given epoch; but when such forces are not balanced, the resulting conflict is prejudicial to the content of the work and to the work as a whole. I should very much have liked to be in a position to present a more realistic achievement: a kind of work which reflects not only refinements and comfort but also a positive collaboration between the architect and the whole society.[6]

The elusiveness of such a collaboration was clear to Niemeyer. Architecture could not be a surrogate for basic social reform: "I believed as I still do, that unless there is a just distribution of wealth reaching all sectors of the populace, the basic objective of architecture, that is its social element, would be sacrificed, and our role as architects only relegated to satisfying the whims of the wealthy."[7]

While this position may seem convenient, Niemeyer's explanation accurately analyzes his own dilemma and that of Brazil. Painfully aware of the persistent presence of Brazil's colonial past and the culture of dependency of which he was an ambivalent part, Niemeyer saw Brazil's socioeconomic, political, and natural environment as a powerful constraining force that architecture more readily reflected than changed. Later he humbly confessed that the contribution of Brazilian architects was profoundly conditioned by a colonial mentality:

We know that our work is chiefly characterized by enthusiasm and creative force. Conditions peculiar to young countries—the lack of long traditions and fixed principles—permit us to take advantage of these qualities to the utmost. Thus, we are aware that our efforts are not based upon great theoretical knowledge, nor upon long or learned experience. We undoubtedly owe the experience that we do have to European culture, which we endeavour to assimilate and adapt to our specific local conditions.[8]

Niemeyer sees architecture as strongly conditioned by the specific yet broadly conceived environment in which the architect works. His earlier free-form extravaganzas mirrored Brazil's social realities, especially the modernizing elite's demand for a distinct cultural identity worthy of international recognition. Powerless to change society, the architect could only hope to break with the legacy of colonial domination in the aesthetic sphere through outrageous innovation that would call attention to Brazilian genius and progress.

Europe humbled Niemeyer and made him aware of Brazil's persisting colonial status in a new manner while it opened his eyes to ways of channeling his frustrated social idealism. If the architect could not change the social structure, he could affect the cultural image of Brazil as a nation-state, reflect the aspirations and talents of its people, and provide poetic symbols for their expression. Fully aware of the shortcomings of his achievements, Niemeyer has sought to justify his formalism by emphasizing his contribution to the formation of a new cultural identity for Brazil: "I see [my works] as positive factors within the Brazilian architectural movement, to which, at a very opportune time, they contributed effectively through their dashing creative spirit, which still characterizes this movement today."[9] Architecture provided a means of creating a new cultural tradition derived from European modernism but rooted in Brazil.

Europe also impressed upon him how monumental architecture functions as a symbol of the great civilization that produces it, and as a permanent expression of cultural values, political aspirations, and artistic genius. The trip showed him the clarity and logic of past styles, especially classicism, against which he had hitherto revolted. Niemeyer's grand tour catalyzed his evolution toward a more monumental, more disciplined but also more plastically and symbolically expressive architecture.

Upon his return to Brazil, Niemeyer began to approach his calling with a greater seriousness. He took on fewer commissions, avoiding purely commercial projects and striving for simpler forms and greater balance among formal, functional, and constructional problems: "I have become interested in compact solutions, simple and geometric, in problems of hierarchy and architectonic character, in the harmony and unity between buildings, and in expressing these qualities not through secondary elements, but rather through the structure itself, appropriately integrated within the original plastic conception."[10] Newly conscious of the immense possibilities of reinforced concrete, he avoided designs composed of multiple elements, which would be difficult to contain within a single, pure form. He stressed that he would not allow the formal discipline of his new approach to degenerate into a "false purism" or the monotonous formulas of an industrial aesthetic, but that it would lead instead to new ideas and innovations.

Niemeyer's new, more disciplined mode—the search for pure and concise form and structure, the interest in architectural hierarchy and character, the desire for a harmonious and unified monumentality and stylistic clarity—adopts elements of the European classicism that he came to appreciate as a result of his travels.

The Museu de Arte Moderna in Caracas The Museu de Arte Moderna (1954–55; figs. 73–76), the unexecuted project that inaugurated this new and fruitful phase of Niemeyer's career, proved that the architect's new interest in formal purity, classical discipline, and compact, volumetric monumentality would not advance at the expense of plastic expression and bold structure.[11] The project also reflects his new interest in architecture as cultural symbol and as grandiose completion of the natural landscape. The dramatic site, on a rocky crag overlooking the city, suggested a dynamic and scenographic solution. As a timeless symbol of the modern movement in Venezuela, Niemeyer proposed an inverted pyramid—a stable classical form turned on its head—in a powerful rhetorical demonstration of the fantastic formal and structural marvels

73. Niemeyer,
project for Museu de Arte Moderna,
Caracas, 1954–55, model

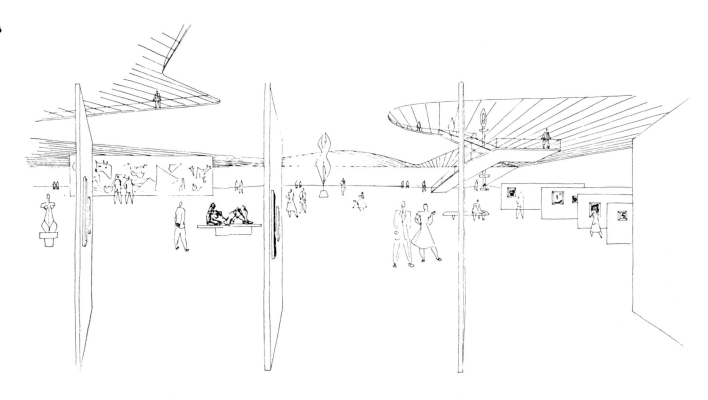

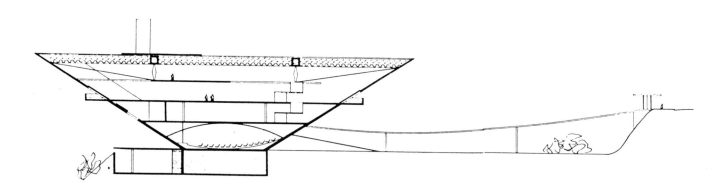

74, 75. Niemeyer,
project for Museu de Arte Moderna,
Caracas, 1954–55, sketch of exhibition area (top)
and section (bottom)

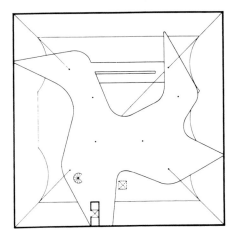

76. Niemeyer,
project for Museu de Arte Moderna,
Caracas, 1954–55, plan of suspended
mezzanine floor

made possible by reinforced concrete. Criticized as a piece of "science fiction" fantasy, the Caracas museum is Niemeyer's first large-scale example of the formal "shock" techniques he would later use to more powerful effect in Brasília.[12] Whereas at Canoas he had sought to neutralize the distinction between site and building, in Caracas and Brasília the neoclassical contrast between a pure geometric form and a vast landscape setting evokes a sense of the surreal and the sublime. The megalomaniac projects of Claude-Nicolas Ledoux and Étienne-Louis Boullée come to mind, but the project is vintage Niemeyer, rooted in his auditorium at Ibirapuera.[13]

New and important in the Caracas museum design are its visual boldness and the architect's interest in the emotional impact of its form and structure. The design evokes a sense of surprise and wonder in the visitor by posing a series of formal contrasts and apparent paradoxes: that of the structure's pure geometric form versus the fluid landscape and of the massive closed exterior versus the apparently open interior, which was to be lighted from the top by a translucent roof covering the largest surface of the pyramid. A suspended ramp would lead visitors into the first-floor foyer, from which other ramps offered access to the exhibition halls, terrace, and auditorium. The structure of the floor slabs of the various levels would be anchored to that of the wall, except for the floor above the large exhibition hall, which, echoing in its contours the free-form canopy of Ibirapuera, was to be suspended with diagonal cables from four hanging columns. Though hardly practical, this ceiling solution was a functionally provocative way to maximize free space and natural lighting, both crucial for a museum. The design exploits both natural and artificial light, with movable aluminum elements and concrete panels that adjust the light to the desired level through an electronically controlled system.

In his speech to the architecture school in Caracas, Niemeyer explained the motives behind this project:

A simple look back to the past shows us that the works that have survived to fill everyone with emotion and surprise are those full of poetry and sensibility. In truth, in front of these monuments of grace and beauty, functional and utilitarian characteristics become secondary for future epochs. Subject to human feelings, stronger than the cold line of theory and reason, architecture continues establishing over the centuries its marks of harmony and beauty. Only artistic creation survives.[14]

77. Niemeyer,
Brasília, begun 1956, general view of main axis
and capitol complex

This new emphasis on emotion, poetry, permanent beauty, and the artist's creative process was to characterize Niemeyer's masterpiece, Brasília.

Much of the polemic surrounding Niemeyer centers on his highly extemporized manner of making architecture, which has outraged some critics. Niemeyer has seemed more inclined than most architects to design from the right side of the brain. Yet his design process is paradoxical, revealing a sensitive balance of rational reflection, empirical analysis, and imaginative intuition. His formal inventions are never the product of caprice but rather of attentive analysis of program, site, and available resources. First he studies the program, economic possibilities, and available technical resources; then he puts the problem aside for a few days, to allow the subconscious to act.[15] Intuition, which intervenes at the invention stage, proceeds from analysis of the objective data. Niemeyer's method and philosophy subtly balance his creative capacity and the material necessities, which orient the solution but do not determine it mathematically. The stage in which the subconscious acts is the most compelling part of the process. Niemeyer's free-form sketches evoke a very real kinship with the automatism of the surrealists. His best mature work is poetic both in its formal methods and in its goal—to evoke plastic emotions.

Brasília: Political and Architectural Foundations The qualities of Niemeyer's new style found powerful expression in the new capital that President Juscelino Kubitschek decided to build in record time beginning in 1956 (fig. 77). Narrowly elected to office without a majority, Kubitschek saw the city as a means of consolidating support from an electorate that had long favored the creation of a new capital. He saw as well a chance to go down in history as the father of a modern and geopolitically integrated Brazil. The project called for forceful leadership that could effectively marshal the diverse interests, motivations, and personalities behind the project into a unified scheme. A new inland capital, it was believed, would shift economic and demographic development away from the Atlantic coast, where Brazil's major cities and most of its population had been concentrated since colonial times. Brasília was thus intended to reverse Brazil's colonial orientation toward Europe and inaugurate a permanent pattern of modern settlement in the vast hinterland. The new city was also seen as an alternative to the inefficient bureaucracy of the old capital, Rio, and as a means of instilling a change in mentality and a corresponding new sense of national identity. As a vehicle for Kubitschek's own campaign of national industrialization and "fifty years of progress in five," Brasília was to serve as both motor and symbol of Brazilian modernization following the trickle-down ideology of diffusionist development. For him, the project's success hinged as much on the

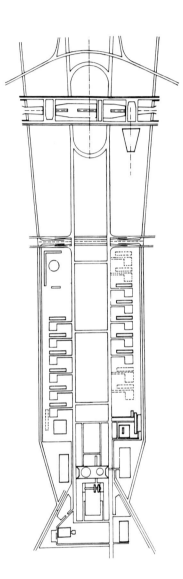

78. Lúcio Costa (plan) and Niemeyer (buildings),
administrative center of Brasília, 1956

9

symbolic image of modernity as on functional or practical considerations. As Norma Evenson wrote: "Kubitschek seems to have sensed that the Brazilian people were ready for an adventure, and that popular imagination would respond to such a grand gesture more readily than to pedestrian and 'practical' enterprises."[16]

Limited to a single five-year term in office, Kubitschek knew that he would have to act quickly—speed was the crucial ingredient in Brazil's new order. He needed above all an architect capable of creatively extemporizing an urban image imbued with poetic expression and powerful modern symbolism. Niemeyer, the obvious choice, was quickly appointed chief architect. He had worked with Kubitschek on several occasions since Pampulha and had established an international reputation and special talent for visual poetry.

In appointing Niemeyer to direct the works with a virtual carte blanche on artistic decision making, Kubitschek repeated Gustavo Capanema's earlier defiance of the Brazilian law that stipulated open competitions for public buildings. But in the face of many protests, Niemeyer wisely refused to develop the master plan for the city, opening it up to a national competition held on March 16, 1957. Yet as a member of the jury, he still had considerable say in the process that named Lúcio Costa's project the winner. The time-honored collaboration between Costa and Niemeyer thus reached its high point in Brasília.

Critics agree that Brasília's aesthetic success largely resulted from the complete accord between Costa's plan and Niemeyer's architecture. The plan—two axes intersecting to form a cross—directly and monumentally asserts a territorial acquisition that reflects the Renaissance ideals of the Iberian conquistadors (fig. 78). Costa described it as "a deliberate act of conquest, a gesture of pioneers acting in the spirit of their colonial traditions."[17] The plan conflated colonial symbolism with Catholic imagery and established a baroque hierarchy of primary and secondary axes that intersect at the modern traffic interchange of a multilane highway. Costa's plan thus recasts traditional elements in modern terms. Whether one sees a bird or an airplane, Costa's "pilot" plan conveys an unmistakable image of flight wholly appropriate to Kubitschek's emphasis on modern speed, as well as his promotion of Brazil's fledgling aviation and automotive industries. Costa labeled the sides of the secondary or residential axis

North Wing and South Wing, reinforcing the metaphor of "flying" the nation into the world of tomorrow.

Niemeyer's architecture takes its cue from Costa's plan and its inherent formal (and social) dichotomies. His designs reflect the creative tension between the European colonial past and an independent Brazilian future that is basic to the project. They respond as well to the modern themes of flight and speed without sacrificing traditional composure and classical equilibrium. It is profoundly ironic that a man personally afraid of flying created some of the most spectacular "airborne" architecture in history. Brasília presented Niemeyer with an unprecedented opportunity to demonstrate his powers of improvisation on a monumental urban scale and his emerging talent for conceptual and formal synthesis. If the project demanded in part the surreal and the sublime, in part the classical and the baroque, Niemeyer rose to all of these challenges in an imaginative and balanced ensemble as plastically expressive as it was unified and disciplined. For all of its shortcomings as a working city, Brasília is a masterpiece of scenography and aesthetic synthesis.

The history and social reality of the city's development have been clarified in a number of penetrating analyses; the entire undertaking met with severe but justifiable criticism.[18] Of concern here is not the deconstruction or reconstruction of Brasília but its significance within the context of Niemeyer's career. The common conclusion that Brasília was an unmitigated failure has blinded us to its many innovations and compelling qualities: it is the purest and most refined vision of the modernist utopia to take actual form. It is more instructive, especially with the benefit of hindsight (which allows us to see through the shallow facades of postmodernism and look deeper into what was vital and important about this failure called modernism) to take a cue from Niemeyer himself, who considered his architecture to be grounded in Brazilian realities. Seen in this way, Brasília emerges as a reflector of a society that sought to change itself by changing its urban image, of the conflicting intentions and aspirations of the city's builders, and of one architect's attempt to harmonize these conflicts through an overriding aesthetic unity that nonetheless expressed the underlying contradictions of the entire project. Even though the rhetoric announced that the new city would create a democratic and egalitarian society, Brasília is a city born of imperial ambitions and as such could only reinforce the existing colonial structures.

Though critics generally assume that Niemeyer intended (and failed) in Brasília to create a social utopia through architecture, the architect was in fact concerned primarily with aesthetic problems, especially how to create unique forms in a unified space. Ever wary of the demagogic politics in which he played a part, Niemeyer, his leftist social idealism notwithstanding, sought to create what

Lionello Puppi has called "an obstinate utopia of beauty."[19] For Niemeyer, artistic creation has become a sublimated form of social action in a world that the architect alone is otherwise helpless to change.

Brasília and the Dialectics of Brazilian Development Brasília's development reflects the dichotomies of the larger Brazilian dilemma, primary among them the modernist utopian idea that a new society could be created through a new architecture promoted by the country's governing and artistic elite. Critics have correctly pointed out that in fact Brasília emerged as a rigidly bipolar city of the governing elite and working-class squatters. The city thus expresses the contradiction between a political reality of absolute authority and the dream of democratic freedom. The denial of Brazilian reality at the heart of Brasília's miraculous foundation myth cast its real builders, the migrant construction workers who came to the city in hopes of a better future, to the periphery. While the city's recruitment campaign emphasized the "democracy" and "frontier solidarity" to come, after the city's inauguration, Brasília's builders were denied a place in the city that they had built. The illusory principle of equality was undermined by the persistence, even accentuation, of the social stratification that characterized Brazilian society.

The Brazilian dilemma is expressed in stark contrast between Brasília's center and its wretched periphery. Even within the monumental core, one observes a typological and formal contrast between the sumptuous modern palaces for the president and key government ministries and the unremarkable, even mundane slabs in which the bureaucrats work. The city thus reflects Brazil's endemic double standard. While seeking to architecturally neutralize class distinctions in the housing blocks of the *superquadras* (large blocks of apartments), Niemeyer actually reinforced the formal and social hierarchies of the new city through a deliberate play of oppositions that privileges a clear architectural (and social) elite.

The greatest challenge of the city and its builders lay in coming to terms with, if not resolving, the social dilemma of Brazilian development. Costa's reference to Brasília's Praça dos Tres Poderes (Plaza of the Three Powers) as the "Versailles of the people" reflects his attempt to harmonize this opposition via rhetorical conflation. Niemeyer's architectural rhetoric also sought to create a new synthesis, transposing the social problems into the more comfortable realm of pure form. As he wrote, "It is strange how the power of beauty makes us forget so much injustice."[20]

While Niemeyer feels that modern times have "opened up to humanity the right and just path of a society free from class distinction, more beautiful and with less suffering," thus providing the "indispensable basis for the modern city wherein the old discrimination can no longer prevail," he stresses that the architect and urbanist alone cannot achieve such objectives:

If we really wish to organize life in human terms, the problem is first to establish a just social basis which guarantees execution of the planning, not allowing it to present a false fantasy or a purely intellectual attitude leading nowhere. It is only thus that planning will prevent discriminatory solutions and the predominance of individualistic interests. Only in this manner will the community—in its impersonal and superior sense—be sovereign, rendering the same possibilities and rights.[21]

In the meantime, Niemeyer seems to suggest, false fantasy and the predominance of individual interests, especially those of the artist, will prevail. Perhaps the greatest tragedy of Brasília is that the city's development has proven Niemeyer's own self-justifying analysis to be correct.

The Dialectics of Form in Brasília Brasília reflects the maturation and discipline of Niemeyer's style under the impact of European classicism while announcing the triumph of the poetic and the surreal. The architecture of Brasília is both a modern reworking of classicism for a stark new environment, that of the Brazilian *sertão* (frontier), and a magical realm of surreal *objets à reaction poetique* (poetic objects)— what Niemeyer called a "space for the imagination." Brasília gave the architect an opportunity to explore a new landscape, to apply his European lessons and newfound seriousness, but also to engage in a project of profound ritual significance for Brazilian culture: the creation of a modern identity and a new cultural tradition based on surrealist inversions of structure and form.

Brasília was from its inception a city of enchantment and illusion. Its magical forms followed its magical function, which was to catapult Brazil out of underdevelopment and into the modern world practically overnight. The project called for a conjurer and a lot of faith. As magician and master of the modernist ritual, Niemeyer was to provide the architectural "tricks" that would prove to the world that Brazil was to be reckoned with, an image of innovative modernity that would sell this idea at home and abroad. Even the process of erecting the city was shrouded in mystery. As James Holston has noted, "The government intended to unveil the built city as if it were without a history of construction and occupation. On inauguration day, it

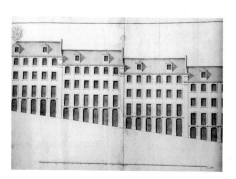

79. Eugénio dos Santos,
design for building facades in
post-earthquake Lisbon, 1756

planned to reveal a miracle: a gleaming city, empty and ready to receive its intended occupants."[22] The city denied the reality of its own history and that of Brazil in favor of future possibilities. As Lawrence Vale summarizes, Brasília's symbolism was "based entirely on future aspirations, a modern tableau set out for a society still enamored by the prospects of mechanization."[23]

Niemeyer's architecture in Brasília addressed two distinct but related design problems: that of the isolated, monumental building in which details are subordinate to the visual effect of the whole, and that of the ensemble, which demands harmony and unity. In an important essay published in *Módulo* in 1959, Niemeyer discusses his ideas about urban unity, which he sees as a major source of beauty in European cities and which he sought to create in Brasília. He was particularly impressed with post-earthquake Lisbon and its effective blending of baroque monumentality, scenographic unity, and classical decorum (fig. 79). Lisbon and Brasília are alike on another level: both are "programmed" cities promoted by enlightened despots who sought to modernize colonial societies by projecting new architectural and urban images. In both cases, uniformity and control are crucial; the control of the demagogue, essential. In the streets of Lisbon, wrote Niemeyer, "The uniformity of structural masses, and the repetition of doors and windows, granite and tile finishes, eaves and color schemes, enhance the stern beauty of the architecture." Modern cities, he finds, "have fallen away from this ancient virtue" and present a "picture of confusion and lack of harmony." He appreciated most of all Lisbon's structural uniformity, the repetitive rhythms of the classical arcade, and the city's juxtaposition of different materials and textures to create a stern effect.[24] This synthesis of structural uniformity, visual rhythms, and formal contrasts is at the heart of the aesthetic unity of Brasília.

The architecture of Brasília combines classical, baroque, and modern. The porticoed palaces bring to mind the Greek temple—common to both is an interest in ideal form, refinement, purity, and equilibrium—but Niemeyer's forms are much lighter, more open and surprising than classically static forms. The palaces resolve as well the dialectic of classical and baroque by reworking the temple theme in a way consistent with the lyricism, formal unity, and scenographic quality of the baroque. Niemeyer sees these classical and baroque qualities through the modernist eyes of the Corbusian discourse and its quest for the surreal.

The Alvorada Palace at Brasília Even before Brasília was a city with a plan, the seeds of Brazil's new society had been sown in the first two buildings of the new capital: the Alvorada Palace (Palace of

80. Niemeyer,
Alvorada Palace (Palace of the Dawn), Brasília,
1956–58, gallery looking toward chapel

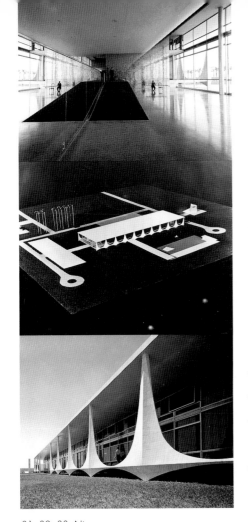

81, 82, 83. Niemeyer,
Alvorada Palace,
Brasília, 1956–58, entrance vestibule (top),
model (middle), and main facade (bottom)

the Dawn; 1956–58; figs. 80–84, 86) and the nearby Brasília Palace Hotel (1957; fig. 85). The Alvorada Palace, the official residence of the president of the Republic, is one of Niemeyer's most widely acclaimed works, the elite of his architectural elite. The isolation of the palace and hotel from the administrative and residential axes of Costa's plan reflects in spatial terms the sociopolitical distance between the governing elite (including their foreign collaborators) and the working classes who built the city. Since Brasília was to project an image of modernity and innovation and to accommodate those who were collaborating in the country's developmental venture, it is not surprising that the first major building to be completed after the Alvorada was a hotel.

The Alvorada symbolizes the importance of the executive initiative of President Kubitschek in spearheading the creation of a new society for Brazil. As Kubitschek wrote, "I chose the name myself. What else will Brasília be . . . if not the dawn of a new day for Brazil?"[25] However, the palace, with its uncomfortable conflation of associations—the dream of a new (democratic) day and the authoritarian palace type—reflects the social dilemma inherent in the planning of Brasília. Moreover, by reasserting the primacy of the executive branch in Brasília's power base, it contradicts the symbolism of the Congress complex, which calls attention to the primacy of the legislature.

In the Alvorada Palace, Niemeyer did, however, usher in a new aesthetic dawn with a modern reworking of a traditional theme—a synthesis of European grandeur and Brazilian grace. He intended to design not just an important residence but "a true palace, imbued with the spirit of monumentality and nobility it called for."[26] For this, he exploited the structure itself to give the building lightness and dignity and to create the impression that it has landed softly on the ground. Niemeyer thus sought the "perfect integrity" of form and structure.

The palace's basic design was set forth in the preliminary anteproject of 1956, which proposed a rectangular glass box between two prominent floor slabs supported by a colonnade whose audacious formal novelty would define the building sculpturally. Subsequent refinements substantially altered the model. The main facade was elongated and its height and width reduced, creating a sleeker and more streamlined building. The colonnade, originally flush with the glass wall, was pulled out to create an external gallery that provides volumetric transition between inside and outside and accentuates the building's sculptural effect. The supports, originally positioned between the two slabs, were lowered to spring from the ground, hiding the floor slab and contributing to the impression of a floating composition. The chapel, separated from the palace in the model, was integrated into the long axis of the composition as an extension of the gallery. An official tribune and a concrete canopy projected for the roof were eliminated, enhancing unity and volumetric purity. The curving artificial stream planned for the front of the palace was removed, eliminating a picturesque element out of place in this solemn and majestic context. Finally, the interior layout was completely modified.

The transition from the anteproject to final design reveals the evolution of Niemeyer's new style based on the triumph of visual considerations above all others. Here the architect increases the plastic unity of the whole by reducing the number of formal elements and focusing on a single motif—the curving colonnade—as the expressive force. As was the Brasília Palace Hotel across the way, the colonnaded gallery of the Alvorada was imagined with the visitor in mind; it enchants with surprising forms and the illusion of floating.

Reflecting the city and the new society that it was to inaugurate, the Alvorada Palace opposes the banal and the extraordinary, the surrealist dichotomy of the real versus the imagined. Formal contrasts and baroque illusionism, not structural truth, characterize its design. The major formal contrast is between the standard International Style glass box and the innovative plastic elements of the colonnade, which are the basis of the building's new artistic identity and cultural symbolism. Like the city itself, the building projects an image based on qualities more apparent than real: the illusion that the building gracefully perches on the ground, supported only by the thin, totally exposed external structure. In fact, this apparently floating box is actually firmly planted on a solid basement hidden by the colonnade. The structural role of the colonnade is much more modest than it appears: the slabs are supported by internal and external supports practically invisible from outside. The sudden interruption of the colonnade at the entrance and the narrowing of the supports toward the top contribute to the impression of extraordinary lightness. The colonnade's forms are thus more decorative and emblematic than architectonic.

This "both-and" architecture contains formal and structural complexities and contradictions. In addition to providing protection from sun and heat, the gallery recalls the colonial plantation house, with its broad veranda and adjoining family chapel. The curving colonnade also inverts the classical arcade and parabolic arches that Niemeyer explored earlier in his career. As in the pyramid of the Caracas

84. Niemeyer,
Alvorada Palace, Brasília, 1956–58, gallery

85. Niemeyer,
Brasília Palace Hotel, 1957

museum, Niemeyer turns the form on its head as part of his modernist game and his search for formal dynamism.

The reflection of the colonnade in the pools in front of the palace and in the gallery floors suggests the illusion of an arcade of parabolas. The colonnade's brilliant whiteness stands out against the green of the glass enclosure, and its gracious forms are reflected, like a series of veils, in pools skillfully placed on either side of the entrance. This transforms the colonnade back into an ethereal, dreamlike arcade of classical antiquity, as if to pose and resolve the duality of ancient and modern. The impression is of a classical dream that has become Brazilian reality, of an ideal and serene beauty subtly translated into the real and the material. Niemeyer's synthesis of the fleeting and the eternal, the charming and the grandiose, levity and security is at its most forceful and compelling here.

The palace presents two fronts, one facing the city and one the garden, both ornamented with sculptures and pools. In front of the building, the bronze statue by Alfredo Ceschiatti—serene, figurative, evoking classical dignity and Olympian calm—blends perfectly with the facade. Behind the palace, the abstract surrealist sculpture by Maria Martins, with its twisted and troubled play of lines and forms, introduces a note of lively contrast against the calm continuity of the colonnade, as Yves Bruand has observed.[27]

The colonnade is the mediating force that integrates and unifies the design's functional and formal dualities. The gallery that it defines provides a transition between inside and outside. The elegant and noble colonnade is also surprisingly light and airy; it synthesizes Brazilian charm with European decorum, classical nobility with baroque plasticity. Niemeyer here offers a modern reworking of the simplicity and purity that he observed in the great works of architectural history. For him, this purity meant the expressive manipulation of a structural idea leading to a new form.

The major criticism of the building came from Bruno Zevi and those in his camp who opposed exclusively "aesthetic" architecture. Such criticism is most applicable to the interior planning, the weakest aspect of the palace despite the efforts of Niemeyer's daughter Ana Maria, who designed it. Baroque illusionism is important in the palace interior, with its ceremonial halls of mirror, rich marble revetments, and metal panels that reinforce the illusionist perspectives of the vestibule and the contrast between interior and exterior. Ramps, galleries, and fluid spaces articulated with glossy surfaces of expensive materials and smooth finishes, like the marble revetments on the exterior, make this the antithesis of Le Corbusier's brutalist Chandigarh.

86 (overleaf). Niemeyer,
Alvorada Palace, Brasília, 1956–58

87. Niemeyer,
Alvorada Palace, Brasilia, 1956–58,
chapel and sculpture (by Alfredo Ceschiatti)

88. Niemeyer,
Alvorada Palace chapel, Brasília, 1957–58

Largely owing to its facade, the image of the building was widely diffused, contributing to Brazil's prestige and international interest in the nascent project of Brasília. On a popular and local level, the colonnade was transformed, throughout the country, into a symbol of the new capital, an effective public relations tool, and a widely copied, even vulgarized image for architects and advertisers. It has been critically acclaimed as one of the most significant monuments of modern times; André Malraux saw it as the first successful attempt to renew the theme of the palace residence since Versailles.[28]

Like Versailles, the palace contains its own private chapel (1957–58; figs. 87–90). This was in part a bow to Catholic tradition, in part an acknowledgment of the political power of the church: a facade of piety in a decadent display of stately sumptuousness.[29] Niemeyer took as his point of departure a study that he had made of Le Corbusier's chapel at Ronchamp in 1955, a year after its completion. He saw in Ronchamp the start of a new, more plastic phase of Le Corbusier's work. Niemeyer's building, however, is lighter, sleeker, and more elegant. While at Ronchamp the visitor is invited to contemplate the building's mysteries without being forced to a precise destination, in his chapel Niemeyer created an organic form that recalls a snail in its shell, a curving passage to the altar carefully controlled by the architect. The use of a colonial statue and gilt wood decoration recalls the contrast of the white exteriors and the dark, rich interiors of colonial churches. The position of the chapel on the side of the palace opened up interesting perspective views and enabled the president to move from one building to the other via a basement passage.[30]

The Planalto Palace, the Supreme Court, and the Praça dos Tres Poderes at Brasília

The Alvorada Palace derives much of its nobility from its isolation, which reflects spatially the sociopolitical distance between the private life of the president and the public city governed. Niemeyer's other major buildings in Brasília, however, carefully express their visual and symbolic interdependence within the city's master plan. In the palaces designed for the government center, Niemeyer above all sought formal unity, classical monumentality, and solemn grandeur while maintaining the ethereal structural lightness and scenographic charm of the Alvorada. The Planalto Palace, seat of the federal government (figs. 72, 91, 92), and the Federal Supreme Court (figs. 94, 95), both designed in 1958 and finished for the inauguration of Brasília on April 21, 1960, are part of the larger urban ensemble of the Praça dos Tres Poderes (Plaza of the Three Powers; figs. 93, 96). The plaza reveals Niemeyer's effort to integrate his architecture

89. Niemeyer,
Alvorada Palace chapel, Brasília, 1957–58

90. Niemeyer,
Alvorada Palace chapel, Brasilia, 1957–58

into a dynamic civic complex of great formal harmony and spatial monumentality. The Praça dos Tres Poderes, a masterpiece of modernist planning, reflects Niemeyer's rediscovery of the fundamental qualities of the classic squares of Europe and his translation of these into contemporary terms.

Niemeyer described his intentions with these words: "In the Praça dos Tres Poderes, unity had been my principal concern. For this I conceived a structural element which acts as a common denominator for the two buildings—the Palácio do Planalto and the Palácio do Supremo Tribunal—and which gives the whole the sense of sobriety of the great squares of Europe, within the scale of values established by Lúcio Costa's magnificent plan."[31]

Seen from above, the plan of the Praça (fig. 78) is roughly a triangle defined by the Congress complex, the Planalto Palace, and the Supreme Court, which together symbolize the three branches of government power: legislative, executive, and judicial. As one approaches from the Congress complex, however, the ensemble unfolds as a series of rectangles dominated by the broad space between the Planalto Palace and the Supreme Court, the two corners at the base of the triangle. The apex is closed off by the Congress complex, with a large reflecting pool and a terrace with imperial palm trees in the foreground. Across from the complex, between the Planalto and the Supreme Court, stands a museum commemorating the city's founding (fig. 97), the only one of the secondary structures on the square planned from the start. The museum, a dramatically cantilevered composition that exemplifies Niemeyer's structural tricks, features a huge bust of Kubitschek surveying the landscape toward the presidential palace beyond the square. The bust is an icon of a president who, mindful of his short term in office, sought to impose his eternal presence on the city that he had created. Sculptures including Bruno Giorgi's *The Warriors*, which memorializes the city's builders, and a monumental dovecot (fig. 98), added during the brief administration of Jânio Quadros (1961), adorn the space.

Like much modern Brazilian architecture, the Praça dos Tres Poderes leads a double existence. As the head of the monumental axis, it is the hierarchical focus of symbolic expression in Brasília. One typically enters the plaza from the side, via the Congress complex, and not from the Alvorada. From a distance, the Congress complex appears between the twin slabs of the administrative towers, with the dome of the Senate and the bowl structure of the Chamber of Deputies on either side (fig. 102). The complex thus presents itself as an acropolis of concrete and glass that, reached by a huge concrete ramp, rises abruptly above the vast graded lawn of the main axis. The sub-level below the concrete esplanade harmonizes the higher levels on either side and the lower level of the plaza behind. Viewed from the esplanade, the composition descends to the lower level of the plaza. The visitor's ultimate destination is this space and no single building.

The Praça dos Tres Poderes interacts vitally with the Congress complex, but it is also an ensemble with a unique architectural dynamic. Its balanced asymmetry, emphasis on volume rather than mass, and shifting visual perspectives reflect Niemeyer's mature Brazilianization of the International Style and the Corbusian discourse, this time on an urban scale. The Praça is a vast *promenade architecturale* in which the major buildings function as sculptural and symbolic *objets à reaction poetique* within a carefully orchestrated, remarkably classical scenography. What Leopoldo Castedo calls the "Baroque prevalence in Brazilian art" is also strongly evident here—from the unified monumentality and multimedia integration of space, architectural form, and sculpture to the plastic vitality of the palace facades. Niemeyer wrote:

In conceiving these palaces, I was also concerned with the kind of mood they would impart to the Plaza of the Three Powers. . . . I visualized it rich in forms, dreams, and poetry, like the mysterious paintings of Carzou, new forms, startling visitors by their lightness and creative liberty, forms that were not anchored to the earth rigidly and statically, but that uplifted the Palaces as though to suspend them, white and ethereal, in the endless nights of the highlands. Forms full of surprise and emotion, which delivered the visitor, if only momentarily, from the insurmountable difficulties with which life burdens man.[32]

91, 92. Niemeyer,
Planalto Palace, Brasília, 1958–60, model (top)
and side view (bottom)

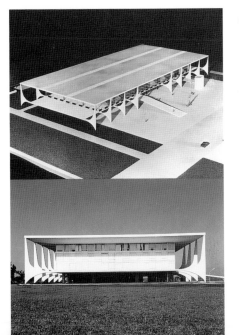

Niemeyer imagined the Praça at night, with its "enchanting and dramatic lighting, against which the buildings stand out in their whiteness . . . floating in the infinite obscurity of the plateau."[33] The reference to surrealist painter Carzou suggests Niemeyer's interest in achieving the magic and mystery of that movement.

While the unity of conception and support systems of the Planalto and Supreme Court guarantee the cohesion and sober grandeur of the Praça dos Tres Poderes, much of the square's dynamism derives from the vital interaction between the buildings and the vast open space around them. The design of the Planalto Palace and Supreme Court recalls that of the Alvorada, in which a glass box is encased in an innovative structural frame, but here the classical feeling is much more pronounced. Both buildings are raised on clearly visible stylobates with roof slabs

93 Niemeyer,
Praça dos Tres Poderes (Plaza of the Three
Powers), Brasília, 1958–60, showing Planalto
Palace and *The Warriors* (by Bruno Giorgi)

projecting over the glass box on all four sides, not just on the front and back. Their broader rectangular proportions are less sleek and closer to Greco-Roman temples, which seem to have been Niemeyer's inspiration. The colonnade of curving supports, perpendicular to the box and not parallel as in the Alvorada, breaks off on the two short sides, creating a pronounced axiality more Roman than Greek and a dynamic fluidity more open to the exterior than the space of classical temples. The orientation of the Planalto, which extends along the whole side of the square and has its main entrance on this facade, is reversed in the Supreme Court, which opens onto the square from one of its short sides, in the manner of a Roman temple. This arrangement creates variety within unity, axial contrast within larger compositional order, while each structure retains its individuality.

The Federal Supreme Court's position on the site, with the statue of Justice by Alfredo Ceschiatti, is such that the approaching visitor perceives the rhythmic succession of its supports in rows, carefully orchestrated for scenographic potential. The perception of sky and clouds through the peristyle accentuates the building's lightness. The fluidity of exterior and interior and the natural fusion of architecture in space are crucial to Brasília's design. The panorama of Costa's esplanade is sculpturally defined by the buildings and enlivened by their support elements. Niemeyer skillfully manipulates angle of vision and distance to reinforce the grandeur and plasticity of the ensemble. Different views of the porticos of each palace escape monotony and reinforce equilibrium based on subtle gradations of scale. The larger Planalto Palace, however, raised higher on its platform than the Supreme Court, commands greater respect and nobility because of its classical monumentality.

The comparison with classical temples should not be pushed too far. The supports of the two buildings fly outward from box and slab like the buttresses of a medieval cathedral (here inverted). The illusion that these graceful supports, perched delicately on the ground, buttress not only the dramatically projecting roof slab but the stylobate (and thus the entire building) as well, accentuates the impression of structural lightness. Niemeyer contradicts structural logic by making his slender buttresses thinnest where they meet the slabs and the ground, the very points where they should be most solid. As in the Alvorada, the structural function of Niemeyer's supports is more apparent than real, more fictive, scenographic, and evocative of the larger modern marvel that is Brasília. Niemeyer relieves the dignified classical monumentality of these buildings with an ethereal, dreamlike image of a structure that is as light as a feather, barely touching the ground, gracefully afloat like the clouds in the sky.

The scenographic framing of Brasília's architectural landscapes and natural skyscapes

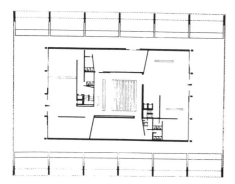

94, 95. Niemeyer,
Federal Supreme Court, Brasília, 1958–60,
ground floor plan (top) and view with statue of Justice
by Alfredo Ceschiatti (bottom)

96. Niemeyer,
Praça dos Tres Poderes, Brasília, 1958–60,
looking toward Federal Supreme Court and Congress
complex

97. Niemeyer,
Museum of the City of Brasília, 1958–60

98. Niemeyer,
Praça dos Tres Poderes, Brasília, 1958–60,
showing dovecot (erected in 1961)

is a major function of the palace colonnades. The floating sculptures of the Congress complex, which contrast dramatically with the flat and barren *sertão* beyond and with the open expanse of the plaza, take on a more human scale and picturesque charm when seen through the frames of the palaces. These bright white, floating objects seem more at home in the clouds than on the flat *sertão*, as do Niemeyer's thoughts on Brasília's evocative sky:

Whenever I travelled by car to Brasília, my pastime was to watch the clouds in the sky. How many unexpected things they suggest! Sometimes they are huge and mysterious cathedrals, Exupéry's cathedrals no doubt; other times, terrible warriors, Roman chariots riding through the air, or unknown monsters running through the winds at full tilt, and more often, because I was always searching for them, beautiful and vaporous women reclining on the clouds, smiling at me from infinite spaces.[34]

Suddenly the shifting winds of the high plains turn the dream into a nebulous nightmare. The fantasy remains unfulfilled: "Soon everything was transformed: the cathedrals vanished in a white fog, the warriors became an endless carnival procession; the monsters hid in dark caves only to emerge even more furious, while the women began to fade and break apart, transformed into birds or black serpents."

To "freeze" a dream and thus make it permanent is an elusive but important goal of Niemeyer's creations at Brasília. Their images, like nature's own forms, remain fluid and changing but find permanence in the architect's imagination. As he confesses: "Many times I thought of photographing all this, so precise were the pictures which I saw. I never did it." Instead he keeps looking at the clouds, trying to "decipher" them "as if searching for a good and expected message." One day, the vision appears again:

On that day . . . the vision was even more incredible. It was a beautiful woman, rosy as a Renoir painting. The oval face, the full breasts, the smooth belly, and the long legs interlaced in the white clouds in the sky. I watched her, in complete rapture, afraid she might suddenly fade away. But on that summer afternoon the wind was probably listening to me and she remained there for a long time, looking at me from a distance, as if inviting me to come up and frolic with her among the clouds. But what I feared had to happen. Little by little my girlfriend started fading away, her arms extending with despair, her breasts flying apart as if separating from her body, her long legs twisting into spirals, as if she did not want to leave that place. Only her eyes continued to stare at me, getting bigger and bigger, full of surprise and sadness—then a larger cloud, dense and black, took her away from me. I kept watching her, disturbed, seeing her struggle with the clouds which surrounded her, seeing her torn by the winds which took her apart mercilessly.

In the end, it is not just her image and her love that elude the poet-architect, but life itself: "I felt how that perverse metamorphosis was similar to our own destiny: we are obliged to be born, grow, struggle, die, and disappear forever, as it was with that beautiful figure of woman."

Niemeyer's Brasília was a quest for eternity in the face of change—a means to express a desire for permanence without denying the inevitability of dissolution and mortality. The only certainties are death and the need for a heroic, permanent, and poetic architecture in which humankind can find redemption in the face of the political turmoil and social injustices of modern history, in the face of a tragic destiny that will not change. If this fatalist view recalls Le Corbusier's "tragic vision," it also reminds us of Malraux's view of the human conquest of destiny through art—the highest form of social action.

The National Congress Complex and the Monumental Axis The emphasis on the monumental axis and its termination as a focal point of the composition invited a scenographic solution that privileged the unity and expressive symbolism of the public buildings. These considerations conditioned Niemeyer's design for the National Congress complex (figs. 99–105). He wrote:

In the National Congress, my purpose was to arrange the plastic elements according to the various functions, giving them a sense of the relative importance required and treating them as a whole with pure and balanced forms. Thus, an immense esplanade, contrasting with the two administrative blocks, marks the horizontal line of the composition, upon which the two plenary chambers stand out. And these, together with the other elements, create that play of forms and shapes which makes architecture what it is, and which Le Corbusier defined so well as "the skillful, accurate, and magnificent play of masses seen in light."[35]

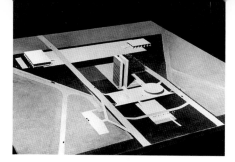

99. Niemeyer,
National Congress complex, Brasília,
1958–60, model

Contrasts and inversions of simple lines—curved and straight—and simple volumes—
rectangular, concave, and convex—are the basis for the design of the complex, which was rooted in
Niemeyer's own experiments in oppositions and inversions: the palace of the arts and the auditorium at
Ibirapuera (1951–54) and the inverted pyramid at the Caracas Museu de Arte Moderna. The architect
also paid attention to function. As Bruand has noted, the form of the Senate cupola and its inversion in the
Chamber of Deputies correspond to the size and character of the two groups working inside: the Senate
dome, of modest dimensions, is firmly planted in a way appropriate for a chamber of reflection; the
Chamber of Deputies's bowl structure, much larger and more revolutionary, resembles a spaceship ready
for takeoff, suggesting the legislative power of an assembly that is to propel Brazil into the future. Yet as
simple inversions of the same volume in different sizes the two forms and functions are intimately related.
Niemeyer offset the imbalance by positioning the twin administrative office towers closer to the Senate.[36]
External appearance, critical for a new capital trying to project a serious image of modernization through
architectural daring, figured above all.

Compared to the unique forms of the Congress complex, the standardized treatment of
the eleven ministry buildings (fig. 110) on the monumental axis calls attention to their secondary status
within Brasília's aesthetic and functional hierarchy. Lined up parallel to one another and perpendicular to
the monumental axis, they are metallic structures, with aluminum-frame windows; the side walls feature
blue-gray ceramic revetments. Weak as individual aesthetic statements, the ministry buildings appear as a
rhythmic succession of staccato stimuli, seen in rapid-fire sequence by speeding motorists on the superhigh-
ways of the motor city: they are the true "backbone" of the city, as one moves from the Praça dos Tres
Poderes to the cathedral and theater.[37]

The Palácio de Itamaraty and the Ministry of Justice The Palácio de Itamaraty (Ministry of
Foreign Relations; figs. 107–9) is the most classical of Niemeyer's Brasília palaces, a building whose
somber character seems wholly appropriate to its serious function. Echoing Le Corbusier's compositions in
the capital complex at Chandigarh, the structure's tall, round arches recall the power and grandeur of the
Roman Empire, equally impressive in architecture and foreign relations. Niemeyer, instead of covering the
concrete structure in flashy marble revetments as he had done in the other palaces, here used the rough,
exposed concrete (*béton brut*) of the sort favored by Le Corbusier and the brutalists. Adapting it to the
Roman theme, Niemeyer layered the concrete to suggest bricks and finished the surface in a light ocher

100. Niemeyer,
Chamber of Deputies and Senate, Brasília,
1958–60

101 (overleaf). Niemeyer,
Chamber of Deputies, Brasília, 1958–60

102. Niemeyer,
National Congress complex, Brasília,
1958–60

103. Niemeyer,
Senate and Chamber of Deputies, Brasília,
1958–60

104. Niemeyer,
Senate, Brasília, 1958–60

105. Niemeyer,
Senate, Brasília, 1958–60

106. Niemeyer,
Palácio de Itamaraty (Ministry of Foreign
Relations), Brasília, 1962–70, roof garden by
Roberto Burle Marx

color to resemble masonry. The concrete thus takes on a warmer tone, and the building appears to be covered with classical revetments.

The building's ponderous force and static equilibrium also distinguish it from the other palaces. The heavy arches, solid and bold, are visually relieved by a reflecting pool upon which the whole seems to float, along with aquatic plants and a Giorgi sculpture. The reflection of the arched facade obscures the floor slab, and the impression of levity and fluidity is accentuated by the almost complete autonomy of the glass box. Much lower in height than the arcade that towers above it, the box seems to float above the pool, increasing the sense of paradox that a tall classical structure could hover so effortlessly over a fluid base. The top floor of the box has a hanging garden, by Roberto Burle Marx, illuminated by a pergola open to the sky (fig. 106). Glass panels rise above the garden level to provide a transparent parapet or balustrade that greatly increases the effect of spatial interpenetration.

The counterpoint to the Palácio de Itamaraty is the Ministry of Justice (fig. 115), in which Niemeyer again used an arcade, this time with suspended waterspouts to surprise and dazzle the spectator and present "architecture and nature hand-in-hand." Niemeyer claims that this was the first "fountain facade" (as opposed to a "facade fountain" such as the Trevi) in the history of architecture.

The National Theater and the Metropolitan Cathedral While Brasília was to be first and foremost a seat of government, Niemeyer's theater and cathedral illustrate his concern for integrating drama and spectacle into his poetic vision of utopian urbanism. Niemeyer claims that he designed the National Theater of Brasília over a Carnaval weekend. The structure actually houses two theaters unified in a single volume, recalling Mies van der Rohe's 1953 project for the National Theater in Mannheim, which has two stages back to back and separated by a movable wall, so that they could function either as separate theaters or as a single auditorium. The mass of Niemeyer's building, with abstract sculptural finish by Athos Bulcão, recalls the form of a Mesoamerican pyramid while reflecting Niemeyer's concern for volumetric purity and sculptural presence (figs. 113, 114).

107. Niemeyer,
Palácio de Itamaraty, Brasília, 1962–70,
first floor plan

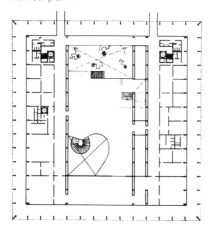

The masterpiece of Brasília, however, is the Metropolitan Cathedral (figs. 111, 112), remarkable for its rich poetic imagery and multiple associations. Niemeyer sought to create a monumental sculpture with an "aerial structure

108. Niemeyer,
Palácio de Itamaraty, Brasília, 1962–70

109 (overleaf). Niemeyer,
Palácio de Itamaraty, Brasília, 1962

110. Niemeyer,
Ministry buildings, Brasília, 1958–60

born of the earth, like a cry of faith and hope."[38] Here the architect's commitment to aesthetic unity and spiritual symbolism was so great that he buried all function underground, so that the structure could reach for the heavens. While the cathedral's crown recalls the passion of Christ and the Queen of Heaven, the building's ribs, buttresses, and walls of glass evoke a Gothic cathedral. Yet its ideal purity of form and essential structure are fundamentally classical. Its evocation of palm fronds and the deep blue-green of a forest canopy are tropical, and its legs, as springy as a spider's, and the weblike formation of the glazing are organic.

The tripartite layout of the cathedral complex consists of a centrally planned sanctuary, a freestanding bell tower, and a separate baptistry connected by an underground passageway. The contrast between the stable, circular plan of the cathedral and the asymmetrical placement of the baptistry and bell tower enlivens the composition. Niemeyer unifies these forms in elevation by making the curving lines of the bell tower's base echo those of the sanctuary ribs, and the tower's spikes point heavenward as does the crown of the cathedral. The dramatically cantilevered slab supporting the bells announces the structural and spiritual magic that is the monument's theme.

Niemeyer's discussion of the project in the 1958 issue of *Módulo* includes illustrations of Greek temples and Gothic churches and a diagram of Gothic flying buttresses. This suggests his interest in the purity of classical structure and the dynamism and lightness of Gothic: a modern evocation of the Greco-Gothic ideal. Impressed with cathedrals both real and surreal (Chartres and the imaginary cathedrals of Saint-Exupéry), Niemeyer observed that church projects belong to the sphere of great structures that through the ages have gauged the evolution of construction techniques. The cathedral project thus challenged him to create a work that demonstrated the advance of modern techniques. Most remarkable is that the cathedral's structural skeleton is the building itself—the purest example of Niemeyer's dictum "When the structure is done, the building is finished." The structure is a circular hyperboloid defined by sixteen boomerang-shaped ribs—really buttresses of parabolic sections turned on end—connected at their bases by a seventy-meter concrete ring serving as the building's foundation and at the top by a concrete slab that holds the rings together and stabilizes the dynamic composition. (Originally Niemeyer had tried to push the laws of structural dynamics too far by proposing twenty-one ribs.)

The cathedral's magic is as much spatial as structural. Placing the entrance gallery in the shadows to prepare the pilgrim for the religious spectacle, Niemeyer maximized contrasts of light and exterior effects, so that the faithful would be transported from this world into a new realm between the

111. Niemeyer,
Metropolitan Cathedral, Brasília, 1959–70,
with statues of apostles by Alfredo Ceschiatti

112 (overleaf). Niemeyer,
Metropolitan Cathedral, Brasília, 1959–70,
showing building after recent painting and reglazing

113. Niemeyer,
National Theater, Brasília, 1958–81,
main facade

cathedral and an infinite space. One must go down into a dark passage in order to be lifted up into the infinite realm of the heavens. This rite of passage parallels the itinerary of the human soul, which must make its way through the depths of darkness before finding salvation and redemption. The cathedral reveals Niemeyer's conception of architecture as a utopian means of spiritually elevating the masses through the play of light on forms and the interpenetration of space. The effect has recently been accentuated by new glazed panels designed by Marianne Peretti (who also did the original ones) and by the treatment of the ribs with a white protective paint.

Art as Redemption Niemeyer's work in Brasília reflects the architect's innermost passion for art as a redemptive force. The architect cannot change society but can transport people who suffer from society's injustices into a higher spiritual realm. The architect's forms are conceived as expressions of hope and as a means to a realm transcending earthly functions. Niemeyer's modernist utopia is thus not of this world: the city and its monuments have an otherworldly surreality that dares only to imagine, to anticipate, what life on this earth could be.

Niemeyer's career also parallels the itinerary of the human soul in a theological sense: he began by revolting against authority and indulging in personal freedom, which led him to both "forbidden things" and an awareness of the prevailing suffering and injustice of the world. This awareness is accompanied by guilt and the need for confession, redemption, and salvation. Art is an offering to obtain redemption from the sins of a world that the architect cannot change. The founding of Brasília was an act of conquest, its plan a diagram of taking possession, its architectural masterpieces a search for personal and cultural redemption. Only through creating great works of art or falling under the spell of their utopian beauty can humankind and civilization hope to be redeemed. Art, an architecture of urban sculptures, *objets à reaction poetique,* takes the place of religion as the new "opiate of the people."

The *Superquadras* and Social Neutralization Brasília marked a cultural rite of passage: it was to lift an entire culture and country out of one stage of development (the premodern or traditional) into another (the mechanized, motorized world of the automobile and the machine.) This project and the vast landscape of the *sertão* also implied a loss—of innocence and of intimacy with the swarming humanity of Rio. Niemeyer has often expressed a nostalgic longing for the very past that was to be

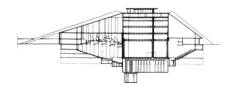

114. Niemeyer,
National Theater, Brasília, 1958–81, section

destroyed—for him, a warm patriarchal past that seem betrayed by the cold abstractions of modern technobureaucracy. Lost in Brasília was the sense of traditional community fostered by the urban street.

Niemeyer himself supervised the development of the *superquadra* neighborhoods. The eleven blocks of superquadra 108 (the first of its type to be completed, 1958–60) include 444 apartments of different types. The source was Le Corbusier's *unité d'habitation*, but Niemeyer lightened and lowered the model to conform with Costa's rule of six-story residential blocks, guaranteeing urban coherence. Niemeyer adopted the volumetric model of the Hospital Sul-América project, with one entirely glazed facade and concrete blades serving as brise-soleils; the back wall, flat, molded, and softly colored, provides a backdrop for the elevator and stair towers. The buildings, arranged back-to-back, have been criticized for their functional flaws: natural ventilation and lighting are impeded.

Contrary to the intentions of its builders, Brasília's design reinforced social stratification and created a rigorous separation of work and living zones. The work zone (the monumental center) clearly expresses the elite trappings of a city for bureaucrats and government officials. In the residential sectors, the designers sought to incorporate people of all income levels into social condensers derived from the Corbusian *unité d'habitation*. Niemeyer wrote of the effort to neutralize social distinctions through basic residential units, the superquadras. The social idealism and determinism implicit in this project were made explicit in a 1963 edition of the official journal of NOVACAP, the state corporation that planned, built, and administered Brasília: "The apartment blocks of a *superquadra* are all equal: same facades, same height, same facilities, all constructed on pilotis, all provided with garages and constructed of the same material—which prevents the hateful social differentiation of social classes; that is, all the families share the same life together, the upper-echelon public functionary, the middle and the lower."[39]

By 1963, however, Niemeyer's effort to achieve social neutralization through standardized housing had been subverted by the traditional polarizations of the society that inhabited the new city. Conflicts arose among the inhabitants over class and status, and new alliances and political mobilization led to the demise of collective housing and the rise of satellite cities. In 1965, following the decision to make most of the apartments available on the open market, rising prices forced the lower-rank civil servants out of the city, leaving the middle-income bourgeoisie in the superquadras and an emergent elite in a residential lakeside area that was supposed to be left undeveloped. The distinction between privileged center and impoverished periphery that characterized other Brazilian cities was reinforced.[40]

The dismal inadequacy of Niemeyer's social condensers suggests that the strength of

115 (overleaf). Niemeyer,
Ministry of Justice, Brasília, 1962–70

116. Niemeyer,
Monument for Juscelino Kubitschek, Brasília,
1980, with sculpture by Honorio Peçanha

117. Niemeyer,
**Pantheon of Liberty and Democracy for
Tancredo Neves,** Brasília, 1985,
with glazed panels by Marianne Peretti

118 (overleaf). Niemeyer,
**Pantheon of Liberty and Democracy for
Tancredo Neves,** Brasília, 1985, with dovecot
on the Praça dos Tres Poderes

his modernism lay in aesthetic rather than social reform. Both the triumph and the tragedy of Brasília reside in the fact that Niemeyer did not allow social pressures to force him to abandon the essentially spiritual project of architecture: the creation of monumental forms symbolic of the power and techniques of the age.

Architecture and Politics in the 1960s Brasília's symbolism reflects the basic contradictions of the society that created it. As Lawrence Vale has noted,

Brasília was an executively directed project designed to demonstrate the power of the legislature in symbol if not in fact . . . but only four years after Brasília was inaugurated, Brazil suffered a military coup. More than 20 years would pass before a semblance of democracy returned. Until the election of Tancredo Neves in 1985, the bold architectural presence of the Congress, front and center, was ironic at best.[41]

Despite this contradiction, Brasília's appeal lies in the wide diversity of readings engendered by its abstract symbolism. Brasília "cultivates Brazilian-ness in only the most abstract of ways. Brasília is Brazilian because it is in Brazil, was designed and built by Brazilians, is named for Brazil and because its overall plan emphasizes the connection of the city to the larger landscape of its place."[42] Its "essential purpose" as Norma Evenson put it, "is to exist where it is." [43] Perhaps this vague abstraction explains how a city "planned by a Left-center liberal, designed by a Communist, constructed by a developmentalist regime, and consolidated by a bureaucratic-authoritarian dictatorship" could have been championed by such diverse interests.[44]

Niemeyer's visual poetry has often led to heated political polemic. The design of Brasília's airport illustrates this. Niemeyer sought a circular terminal to accentuate unity, but the military government insisted on a linear design it considered more practical. In the end ideological, not functional, differences were at stake: "A communist architect's place is Moscow," the military charged. Similar problems arose with the construction of the 1980 commemorative monument to Juscelino Kubitschek (figs. 116, 119, 120). When Niemeyer proposed that a small statue of the former president be placed in a crescent-shaped frame atop the monument, the military saw a hammer and sickle, and a vicious press scandal resulted. Such political problems with the rightist military regime eventually forced Niemeyer out of Brazil, where he would produce his exile architecture.

Brasília, however, and the Praça dos Tres Poderes in particular, remains Niemeyer's ritual realm. He has overseen all architectural and sculptural additions. The base of the plaza's triangle, left open in the original design, was filled in 1987 with Niemeyer's Pantheon of Liberty and Democracy dedicated to Tancredo Neves, who died only weeks after assuming office in 1985 (figs. 117, 118). The white sculptural structure in Niemeyer's late free-form mode, with stained glass by Peretti, evokes the biomorphic image of doves taking flight and is thus consistent with the airborne theme of Brasília and the ethereal floating palaces of the plaza.[45] The plaza has become a ritual showcase of Niemeyer's almost mythic endurance in the face of Brazil's ever-changing political situation.

119. Niemeyer,
Monument for Juscelino Kubitschek, Brasília,
1980, exhibition panel showing journal clippings

120 (overleaf). Niemeyer,
Monument for Juscelino Kubitschek, Brasília,
1980

Niemeyer Abroad

While Brasília was unquestionably the greatest professional opportunity of Niemeyer's career, his twelve years of travel and work in Europe, the Middle East, and North Africa between 1962 and 1974 brought him an important chance to advertise the innovations of Brazilian modernism and to achieve further international recognition. Niemeyer describes his journey as "a new experience": accompanied by an assistant and a model maker (German engineer Hans Muller and French designer Guy Dimanche), he set out to cover the world and design a diversity of projects "in record time."[1]

The context for Niemeyer's travels were the political events of the early and mid-1960s, especially the coup of April 1964, which replaced left-of-center President João Goulart with a rightist military regime. The coup undercut Niemeyer's official government patronage and prompted his more vocal opposition to the class-based conflicts that characterized this unsettled period of Brazilian history. During the 1960s and early 1970s, the military police brought Niemeyer in for questioning on several occasions and once even ransacked his office in Rio. "What is it you Communists want?" they demanded. "To change society," Niemeyer calmly responded.[2] Blacklisted and ultimately exiled from his homeland, the architect fortunately found support and patronage from several foreign governments, most notably France and Algeria. President Charles de Gaulle created a special decree allowing Niemeyer to work in France, where he benefited from the patronage of Minister of Culture André Malraux and the French Communist Party. Finally, in 1972 Niemeyer opened an office on the Champs-Élysées in Paris. The Algerian dictator Houari Boumédienne, impressed with Niemeyer's work for Kubitschek in Brasília, offered the architect similar preferential treatment. Only the Americans, paranoid about Niemeyer's communist affiliations, closed the door to him, twice refusing him entrance visas and preventing him from accepting an honorary position at Yale University. One can only speculate about the potential impact of Niemeyer's presence on America's stalwart architectural academy.

Niemeyer's earlier overseas journeys had taken him to New York, first with Costa to design the Brazilian Pavilion at the World's Fair in 1939, and second in 1947, when he was invited to participate in the design of the United Nations headquarters, a project overseen by Wallace Harrison and Max Abramovitz. In 1954 he traveled to Venezuela and Europe and made more frequent trips after 1962. After Brasília, Niemeyer traveled back and forth between Europe, Africa, the Middle East, and Brazil, working simultaneously on projects at home and abroad. Though many of these projects remained unexecuted, Niemeyer's work of the 1960s and 1970s was important in divulging Brazilian achievements and furthering the evolution of his free-form mode on the ensemble and urban scales.

The United Nations Headquarters in New York Niemeyer's period of international adventure and innovation in the 1960s and 1970s was foreshadowed by his experience in New York and his work on the U.N. complex in the late 1940s. His United Nations project reveals his early transformation of the Corbusian discourse on the level of the urban ensemble. It also illustrates the dynamics of his working relationship with Le Corbusier. Niemeyer's role in the design process was more significant than most writers have acknowledged. William Curtis, in his standard textbook on twentieth-century architecture, for instance, forgets to mention that Niemeyer was even involved.[3] The project was of course a matter of pride for Le Corbusier, who had suffered rejection over his proposals for the League of Nations in Geneva. The U.N. headquarters appealed to him for its worldwide symbolic import, and he was determined to go down in history as its designer. Niemeyer, on the other hand, saw the project as a collaborative venture in which a design board of architects would work together to develop the best solution.[4]

121, 122, 123, 124. Niemeyer,
sketched plans for the United Nations,
New York, 1947, Le Corbusier's Scheme No. 23A
(top), Scheme No. 32 (upper middle), collaborative
Scheme No. 23A–32 (lower middle), and Scheme
No. 32 (bottom)

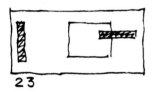

23

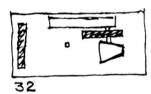

32

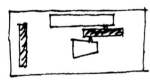

23-32

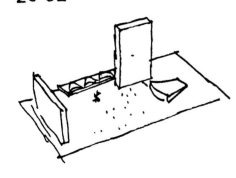

Niemeyer relates that on the day he arrived in New York in February 1947, Le Corbusier called his hotel to arrange a rendezvous on a corner of Fifth Avenue. Le Corbusier told Niemeyer that he felt that his own project was misunderstood and appealed to Niemeyer not to make matters worse by submitting a new design. Niemeyer agreed and remained in his hotel room to avoid the daily committee meetings. One afternoon, Harrison called him into his office and said: "Oscar, I didn't invite you here to collaborate with Le Corbusier, but to present your own solution like everyone else." The committee needed Niemeyer's contribution before it could make a final decision. Within three days, his project was ready.[5]

Le Corbusier's Scheme No. 23A (fig. 121) proposed three distinct blocks, one for the Secretariat, one for an office annex, and one for the General Assembly and Conference Building. Niemeyer's Scheme No. 32 (figs. 122, 124, 125) kept the Secretariat in the place proposed by Le Corbusier but made several modifications to accentuate the ensemble's visual impact. He separated the General Assembly from the Conference Building and placed it alongside the Secretariat. For the Conference Building he created a low block on the edge of the river. These changes opened up the ensemble and created the United Nations Plaza.

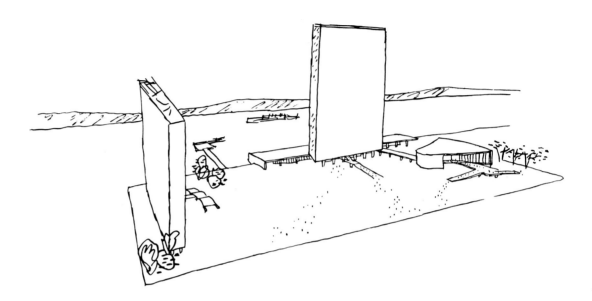

125. Niemeyer,
sketches for the United Nations, 1947,
Scheme No. 32

While the Secretariat clearly derives from the concrete slab of the Ministry of Education and Health Building, it also anticipates, in its glazed geometric purity, the administration towers of Brasília. The U.N. Plaza looks forward to the spatial dynamism of the Praça dos Tres Poderes.

Niemeyer's project was selected by the committee the following week, but Le Corbusier promptly asked Niemeyer to approve his modification to the design, insisting that the General Assembly be at the center because it was the principal element of the complex. Although convinced that the plaza he had created added greatly to the monumental character of the design, Niemeyer compromised with Le Corbusier: the two projects were brought together into one, Scheme No. 23A–32 (fig. 123). Niemeyer wrote that he did this to please Le Corbusier, "the man who had created the basis for an entire school and whom we were accustomed to admire and defend."[6] The U.N. complex went through a number of subsequent design changes that cannot be analyzed here. But as Victoria Newhouse has concluded: "It was Oscar Niemeyer who provided the link between the French architect's design and what was ultimately realized at the U.N.[7]

Abramovitz remembers well the events leading up to the selection of the final design. In 1991 he observed:

Of course the man who tried to dominate everything was Le Corbusier. He was really trying to run the whole thing. . . . Actually what happened is that when Corbu saw Niemeyer, he expected him to be his yes-man—he expected him to work for him. Harrison tried to keep everything under control. . . . Anyway, somewhere along the line, Niemeyer started to understand the program. . . . We knew about Niemeyer and started to respect him a little bit, but then after a week or two he stopped showing up at the meetings. Finally Wally said to me, "Why don't you go over to his hotel and find out what's going on." He stayed in his hotel; we don't know what went on there. So I went up there and the guy that was with me asked him to come back—why was he away? I thought he was sick or something. Niemeyer said, "No, I don't want to come." He was tired of fighting off Le Corbusier, who was trying to make him do what he wanted to do. We told him we wanted him, but he was being used by Corbu and he wasn't strong enough to say, "Keep out of my way, don't bother me." I think his courage occurred after we made him come back. He said one time after he came back, "I admire Le Corbusier as an artist and an architect, but I don't admire him as a man." Corbu was very tricky and caused us a great deal of problems.

Then Niemeyer started to make a few sketches. We decided that Le Corbusier's solution, which he had fought for for a long time, had to be pulled apart. There were several problems: the site, the orientation, and so on. The group decided that we couldn't live with Le Corbusier's solution. Niemeyer started to make his own little sketches. He's a fascinating draftsman. I've never seen that ability before. He visualizes it in his mind and starts drawing, and he doesn't take his hand off his sheet until the whole damn thing is drawn up and you see a composition in front of you. Well, by God, we started to respect that. Then what happened was that we made minor variations to the different parts. . . . Slowly, when he saw that we were behind him, he quietly kept on going. Niemeyer never came on strong, but his sketches talked—much louder than we realized.

Slowly the thing evolved. There was a period of kicking ideas around, and slowly we caught ourselves using more of the input of Niemeyer than almost anybody else. It was all around that kernel of Niemeyer's idea—the positioning of things.

We were slowly heading in the direction of Niemeyer's Scheme No. 32. I was in the drafting room, where we had all the sketches on the wall and the models on the tables. Corbu came into the room and took down something like this [pointing to a photo of Niemeyer's Scheme No. 32], disappeared somewhere, then came back in, made his sketch, which he called 32A, and signed his name to it. He just couldn't stand it.[8]

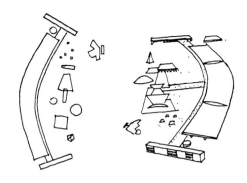

126, 127. Niemeyer,
International Exposition Complex, Tripoli,
1962, sketched plan and elevation

Niemeyer in 1947 was a youthful and impressionable artist whose admiration for his imposing mentor, Europe's greatest architect, was thoroughly understandable. Niemeyer in 1967 was a different man. Brasília had achieved world renown, and Le Corbusier had passed away. Niemeyer emerged from beneath Le Corbusier's shadow to impose his own modernist conquest on the world. Unlike Le Corbusier's quest for universality, however, Niemeyer's was a decidedly Brazilian venture marked by improvisation and structural feats. Niemeyer wrote that his goal in this period was to show the world the innovations of Brazilian architecture and engineering. This corresponded to a period in which Brazil (under President Jânio Quadros) was particularly concerned with foreign affairs and the continued projection of an image of Brazilian modernity.

Planning Projects in the Middle East and North Africa, 1962–69 Niemeyer's period of travels began in 1962 when he received a telegram from the Brazilian ambassador in Beirut inviting him, in the name of the government, to design a permanent international exposition complex for the city of Tripoli. Niemeyer's first task was to define the layout of an ensemble of pavilions and annexes (figs. 126–28, 130, 131). He wrote that his intention was to create a complex that "rejected the normal type of exhibition which, repeated year after year around the world, consisted of isolated pavilions . . . (that) created a disagreeable confusion."[9] Instead, he proposed to encompass the different national pavilions under one huge, flat concrete roof similar to the canopy of Ibirapuera. This horizontal platform would discipline the ensemble from a plastic point of view, unifying and distinguishing the different forms at the center. These included a Lebanese Pavilion, a space museum, an experimental theater, an open-air theater, a nature museum, a fountain, and a restaurant. On the far end of the roof slab were an entrance portico and tourist hotel. The proposed pavilions were to display "the great themes that impassion the contemporary world: spatial experiences imbued with beauty and mystery; the evolution of nature and its perspectives; theater, music, cinema, etc." While the Lebanese Pavilion was to present the traditions and progress of Lebanon, Niemeyer seemed to appreciate those aspects of Lebanese culture and especially nature that were most like Brazil: the "marvelous sea" he espied from his hotel room in Beirut, he wrote, evoked memories of his homeland.[10]

Back in Brazil during the administration of Goulart (December 1962–March 1964), Niemeyer continued his work in Brasília, concentrating on the

128. Niemeyer,
International Exposition Complex, Tripoli,
1962, pavilions under construction

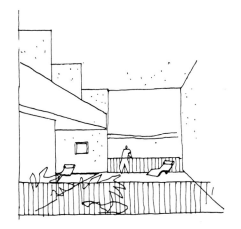

129. Niemeyer,
Ideal City of Neguev, 1964,
sketches of residential blocks

Palácio de Itamaraty and the University of Brasília, where he introduced a centralized plan that made use of prefabricated elements.[11] This was a period of social unrest and great hope for Niemeyer and his leftist comrades, who supported the social reforms and nationalization policies of Goulart. Niemeyer received the news of the military coup of 1964 in a hotel in Lisbon. Deeply depressed by the turn of events, he proceeded to Israel, where, at the expense of a businessman named X. Federman, he closed himself off in a hotel room in Tel Aviv for six months. During this time he worked on several projects, the most important of which were the Ideal City of Neguev and the University of Haifa.[12]

The unexecuted project for the desert city of Neguev reveals Niemeyer's approach to the problem of the ideal city (fig. 129). Unlike the universal proposals of Le Corbusier, Niemeyer's highly theoretical project was not presented as a definitive solution for all places and times. Instead, he emphasized that the project was conditioned by the specific physical context of the desert surroundings and was to be adaptable to the inhabitants' individual needs. The design also reflects the architect's personal preference for small- to midsize medieval cities, whose urban offspring he found in the hinterland of his native Brazil. Such settlements, he wrote, "were more on the scale of man and [fostered] human solidarity which the great metropolis has destroyed."[13]

The Neguev plan was essentially a Corbusian vertical garden city designed to accommodate sixty thousand on the urban scale of a medieval town. Conceived as a pedestrian park that would eliminate asphalt streets, traffic congestion, and the problems of access created by the automobile, the city's compact layout was to facilitate walking between work, home, and school and to maximize open space for easy circulation and parks and gardens. The town hall, civic center with a covered garden, and buildings for commerce and entertainment, designed with prefabricated modular concrete elements, were placed at the center. Around these Niemeyer laid out the residential units, cultural and educational sectors, and zones for sports and leisure facilities. A peripheral ring road distributed traffic into the center. The plan completely separated pedestrian and vehicular traffic, with a large central esplanade that would provide parking for ten thousand cars and serve as the city gateway and focus traffic control. Beneath the esplanade Niemeyer projected a transport hub with service facilities and direct linkage via ramps to the town's commercial and recreational zones, which also featured underground

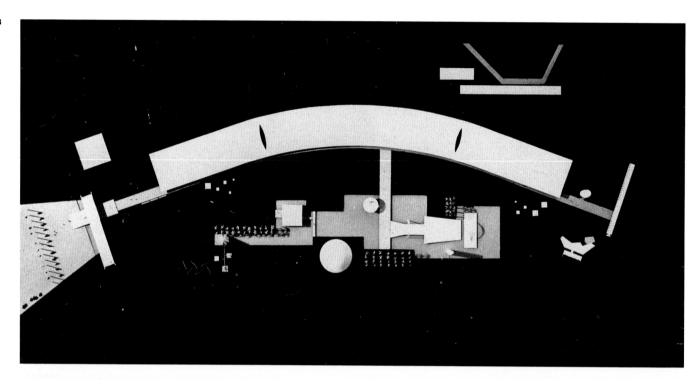

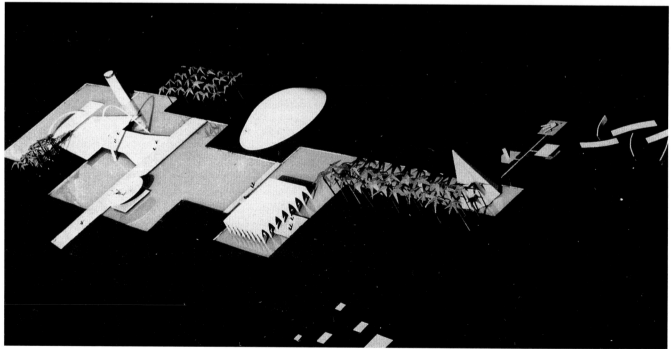

130, 131. Niemeyer,
International Exposition Complex, Tripoli,
1962, model

132. Niemeyer,
University of Constantine, 1969–77

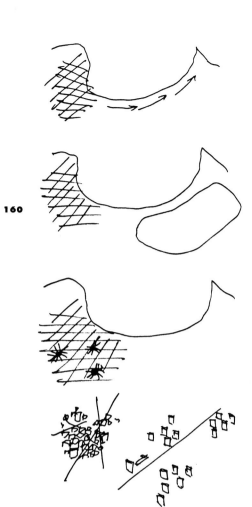

133. Niemeyer,
urban development plan for new Algerian
capital, 1968, sketches showing lines of
urbanization near Algiers

service streets to guarantee fluid and independent circulation.[14] Niemeyer's housing solution for Neguev was conditioned by his double agenda of intimate pedestrian scale and efficient traffic circulation. The only way to guarantee both was through closely spaced Corbusian vertical blocks. Low horizontal blocks of four to eight stories would have destroyed the pedestrian scale and high-density pattern by requiring more buildings and more horizontal space. Niemeyer projected eight groups of four blocks, thirty to fifty stories high, with apartments of the Corbusian vertical Citrohan type. This, Niemeyer wrote, would enable the inhabitants to "avoid dust, sandstorms, and the reflection of solar radiation off the desert floor" and offer the chance "to breathe purer air and to admire the splendid panorama offered by the Neguev."[15] Each apartment would have as its core an exterior living room, a double-height garden terrace connected on one side to the building's entrance corridor and opening on the other to a view of the desert. Niemeyer emphasized that the inhabitants would have ample freedom to adapt the apartments, the functions of the rooms, and the interior decor according to personal preference. Only the basic layout was standardized.[16]

Niemeyer saw the Neguev plan as a utopian tool for the civilization of the remote desert following the diffusionist ideology of Brasília. Though he spoke of including industry and agriculture in carefully planned urban zones, the specific economic basis of the city was not made clear. Nor were issues of environmental feasibility such as water supply addressed. Neguev was conceived as a self-contained, self-referential urban system like the garden-city satellites of Ebenezer Howard. The Neguev nucleus, Niemeyer stressed, was not expandable; rather, it could only be repeated, "multiplied into infinity along the great routes of communication . . . bringing with it into the hinterland life and progress in a organized and disciplined form." In this way, humankind was to be "integrated into the hostile nature of the desert which [it] desires to correct and render agreeable."[17]

Another opportunity to apply Niemeyer's Corbusian planning ideas in a non-European context came in 1968, when Houari Boumédienne commissioned him to design a new university for the city of Constantine and an urban development plan for the Algerian capital. Although the Algiers plan was not executed, it reveals the evolution of Niemeyer's free-form approach on a large urban scale. Well

134. Niemeyer,
proposed civic center for new Algerian capital,
1968, model and photomontage

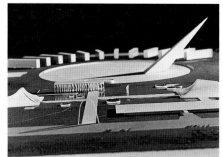

aware of Le Corbusier's earlier projects for Algiers, Niemeyer took as his point of departure Le Corbusier's proposal for a "horizontal" or "route" city that followed the curving contour of the Algerian coastline. Niemeyer was interested in creating a non-Eurocentric project, or at least one at home in its Arab cultural context. Rather than replanning the ancient core of Algiers, he proposed to construct a new city along the coast in the direction of Cape Matifou, following the spontaneous development already in progress.[18] Niemeyer's free-form planning thus reinforced the informal or organic patterns of Arab urbanism.

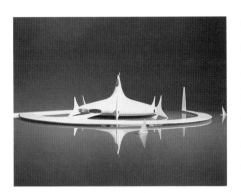

135. Niemeyer,
project for a floating mosque for new Algerian capital, 1968, model

Niemeyer preferred creating a new, semiautonomous capital city rather than replanning the old because he believed that the imposition of the new on the old would overburden Algier's already stressed infrastructure and thus compromise the progress that the "city of the future" was to bring the Algerians. The principal urban nuclei of his new city—the business center, administrative complex, cultural sectors, and housing zones—were laid out along the coast and separated by green zones (fig. 133). The focal point was the civic plaza, a large circular space around which were positioned, on one side, twelve low blocks for ministries, and on the other, an ensemble consisting of the presidential palace, the ministry of foreign relations, and a council chamber. The curved surfaces of the palace and ministry were to recall the forms of Arab tents (fig. 134), and the ogival arcade of the council chambers, as well as the parabolic entrance arch between the sea and the ensemble, echoed traditional Islamic architecture. At the center of the plaza Niemeyer projected a monument to the Algerian revolution, a "symbol of an epic period of liberation and progress." Conceived as an inclined pyramid-obelisk 150 meters high, the monument speaks as well of the march of time and human affairs, like some cosmic solar clock in an immense and mysterious space.[19] Niemeyer also planned a mosque "perched on the sea," connected to the shoreline with a floating ramp bridge that encircled the building, protecting it from waves. The mosque was to float above the water, supported by curving buttresses that recall those of the cathedral at Brasília (fig. 135). With this design, Niemeyer hoped "to introduce in Algeria a different and more daring architecture, capable—like Brasília—of encouraging tourism" and symbolizing the modern epoch for Algerians. Boumédienne described the mosque as "revolutionary," but he was not impressed enough to carry it out.[20]

Niemeyer's proposals for the University of Constantine, however, met with greater approval (figs. 132, 136, 137). When Boumédienne and Minister of Education Taleb submitted a

136 (overleaf). Niemeyer,
University of Constantine, 1969–77, library

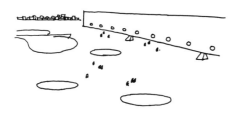

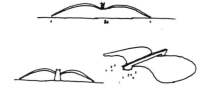

137. Niemeyer,
University of Constantine, 1969–77, sketches

program calling for some forty buildings, the architect responded characteristically: he reduced the number of structures to two principal monoblocks, one for classrooms, the other for research laboratories, both making extensive use of modular elements of precast concrete. Such a solution, foreshadowed in his proposals for the university complexes at Brasília (1960), Haifa (1964), and Cuiabá (1968), reflected his personal commitment to academic centralization and his desire, evident as early as the Obra do Berço, to condense a complex of functions into an integrated formal unity. Niemeyer also stressed that, compared to a design with multiple structures, his simplified solution was more economical in cost of infrastructure and maintenance, more respectful of the hilltop site, and more conducive to the interaction of students, and thus pedagogically superior. The two blocks were to be connected to several secondary structures—auditorium, library, dormitory, administrative offices, and sports facilities—via a network of underground passageways. These passageways, however, along with the dormitory, were not executed for financial reasons.[21] Though compromised by hasty execution and financial problems, the university was inaugurated in 1972. Critics have noted the lyrical, *parlant* quality of the buildings.[22]

Projects in Europe, 1967–78 The works that Niemeyer carried out in Europe in the post-Brasília period are variations on and refinements of familiar themes, with a greater emphasis on sculptural freedom and the spatial context of the city: a logical outgrowth of his experiments in the fifties and his work in Brasília. The headquarters of the Communist party in Paris (1967–80), which Niemeyer considers one of his best works in terms of quality construction, sets the Senate dome of Brasília in front of the meandering slab of the Copan Building, but on a much smaller scale and with a more intimate fusion to the site (figs. 138, 139). During his second visit to France in 1965, Niemeyer had been approached by the party chairman about bringing together the party's various offices, then dispersed throughout the city, into a centralized headquarters. A year later, on his third trip to France, he met with Georges Gosnat of the party's central committee for final negotiations on the project, which was begun in 1967. During the first phase of construction Niemeyer was assisted by Brazilian architect José Luis Pinho and French architects Jean de Roche, Paul Chemetov, and Jean Prouver.[23]

The site chosen for the Partie Communiste Française (PCF) building, an already limited space in the northeast section of the city on the Place Colonel Fabien, had been cut back even more by the expansion of the adjacent Boulevard de la Villette. Niemeyer proposed an eight-story block with an

138. Niemeyer,
Communist party headquarters, Paris,
1967–80

139 (overleaf). Niemeyer,
Communist party headquarters, Paris,
1967–80

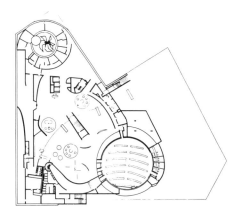

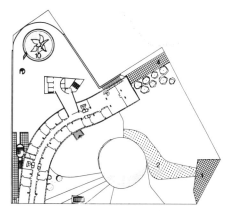

140. Niemeyer,
Communist party headquarters, Paris,
1967–80, main floor plan

141. Niemeyer,
Bourse de Travail, Bobigny, 1972–80, section

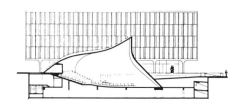

undulating plan to exploit the irregular site. Through skillful grading and layering of the earth, the main block appears to float above the ground (without the use of pilotis). As in the cathedral of Brasília, Niemeyer again buried the building's major functional spaces, a worker's hall and an auditorium (expressed by the dome), to call attention to the juxtaposition of discrete sculptural objects in free space. Niemeyer argued that his solution provided ample room on the ground level, which was left almost completely free of structural elements.[24] Indeed, his skillful manipulation of the functional elements enabled him to turn a problematic site into an open sculptural space that contrasts dramatically with its drab Parisian neighbors (fig. 140).

The accentuation of formal contrasts—the dark glass of the office block against the white concrete of the dome—was key in the PCF design and a constant theme in Niemeyer's oeuvre. He took it up again, to less dramatic effect, in the 1972 project for the Bourse de Travail (Workers' Union Headquarters) for Bobigny (a suburb of Paris), in which a shell-like auditorium of striated concrete is set against a five-story block on pilotis (figs. 141–43). As Gilbert Luigi has observed, the Bobigny auditorium is a strange "sculptural event" that calls attention to the banality of the neighboring buildings: "In this context, the monument resounds with the glory of the working world and of the trade unionism of which it is the house and to which it is dedicated."[25]

Niemeyer's headquarters for the Mondadori Publishing Group outside Milan (1968–75; figs. 144, 146–48) is another example of the architect's ability to rework old themes on different sites to achieve new and surprising effects. Giorgio Mondadori commissioned Niemeyer to design a building that would accommodate the multiple functions of the expanding publishing house, which had outgrown its offices in central Milan. The locale was an ample site near Segrate, a suburban center about fifteen kilometers from Milan, near the Linate airport and with easy access to the highway leading to Verona, where the company's typographic offices were located. The program called for a unified and monumental solution that communicated the stalwart character and prestigious publishing tradition of the company's founder, Giorgio's father Arnaldo. The Palácio de Itamaraty in Brasília, with its arcade and reflecting pool, was the point of departure.[26]

Niemeyer proposed two solutions. The first called for two separate,

142. Niemeyer,
Bourse de Travail, Bobigny, 1972–80

143. (overleaf). Niemeyer,
Bourse de Travail, Bobigny, 1972–80

144. (second overleaf). Niemeyer,
Mondadori Building, Segrate, near Milan,
1968–75

145. Niemeyer,
Mondadori Building, near Milan, 1968–75,
interior of office and arcade

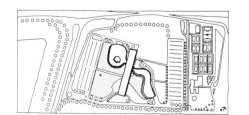

undulating blocks laid out parallel to one another. The second design, preferred by Niemeyer and ultimately adopted, was a larger single block that brought together all of the administrative offices in one building—a floating, five-story prism of glass and steel encased in a system of tall arches as in the Itamaraty. Here, however, Niemeyer's proposal for an arcade with arches of varying width gave the facade an entirely different, free-form rhythm and posed a formidable challenge for the engineers responsible for the structural calculations (Luciano Pozzo, Antonio Nicola, and Glauco Campello). A total of forty-four arches of six different widths march across the front and rear facades, creating a varied and highly musical rhythm recalling that of Le Corbusier's monastery of La Tourette at Eveux (1953–59). Niemeyer's solutions in the Palácio de Itamaraty and Mondadori Building are both anticipated by Le Corbusier's High Court at Chandigarh (1951–56).[27]

Niemeyer placed the secondary functions—restaurants and shops for the employees—in a roughly circular, sculptural structure with an open plaza at its center. The structure appears to float in the artificial lake in the front of the office block. Behind the main block lies a third structure, the plan of which resembles the leaf of a river mangrove, which contains the company's editorial offices. The three structures connect on the ground floor to the main entrance hall. A long ramp bridge connected to the hall offers access to the complex from the parking area, over the artificial lake and past the monumental sculpture by A. Pomodoro.

Niemeyer placed a premium on the articulation of a fluid, flexible, well-lit interior space as open as possible to the exterior. The openness of the interiors, with their hanging gardens, in large measure results from the structural solution: Niemeyer hung the floors from the external concrete frame via vertical cables, leaving the ground beneath the glass box completely free of structural elements.[28] The office interiors feature open or false ceilings composed of blades of white aluminum aligned in an orthogonal pattern, creating a variegated surface rich in light and shade, which also hides the building's technical and electrical infrastructure (fig. 145).[29] The building's continuous windows are double-paned (bronze toned on the exterior and clear on the interior), with a layer of air between for thermal and acoustical security. Precisely because of the technological sophistication that went into the PCF and Mondadori headquarters, Niemeyer considers his European works generally superior to those carried out elsewhere. Niemeyer wrote that the Mondadori Building "proved to the entire world that technical progress must not paralyze the imagination, and that

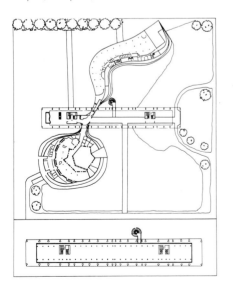

146, 147, 148. Niemeyer,
Mondadori Building, near Milan, 1968–75,
site plan, floor plans, and section

149. Niemeyer,
Maison de la Culture, Le Havre, 1972–82

150. Niemeyer,
Maison de la Culture, Le Havre, 1972–82

151. Niemeyer,
Maison de la Culture, Le Havre, 1972–82

152. Niemeyer,
Maison de la Culture, Le Havre, 1972–82

lyricism, invention, and fantasy must remain present because they are the very essence of architecture."[30]

This statement sets the tone for the formal innovations of the cultural center Niemeyer designed in Le Havre (1972–82.) The program of the Maison de la Culture originated with de Gaulle's minister of culture, André Malraux, who defined the institution: "One of those special places meant to promote the meeting of the general public, excluding no one, and for cultural benefits of every kind and of the highest standard, from the past and present."[31] Earlier, in 1961, Le Havre's cultural center, France's first, had been installed in the city's Musée des Beaux Arts; in 1967 it moved temporarily to the theater in the town hall. The ideology behind the French politics of popular culture, "the right to culture for everyone," was in keeping with Niemeyer's communism, and he enthusiastically espoused cultural accessibility as a goal. He later wrote: "Of all my foreign projects, the Cultural Center of Le Havre is, without doubt, the one representing the most significant social content."[32] Niemeyer's Maison de la Culture (figs. 149–56), commissioned and financed by the municipality, was the culmination of a long struggle on the part of the politicians and citizens of Le Havre to express the city's tarnished cultural identity appropriately, reflecting its status as a major economic hub and France's largest Atlantic seaport. The city had been heavily bombed during the Second World War and later reconstructed by Auguste Perret

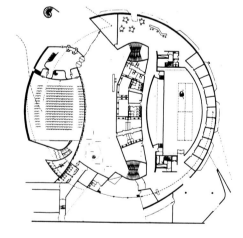

in a monotonous, stripped classical style, but as late as 1956, according to Patrick Fils, "culture was practically nonexistent in Le Havre."[33] As he wrote, "Le Havre's Maison de la Culture was the first in France. . . . Twenty-one years later, its rebirth will give the city a political medium, in accordance with the wishes of its elected officials, create a meeting place for the Havrais, and make of our city a new beacon for the entire country."[34]

Niemeyer's solution reflected his sensitivity to Le Havre's climate, history, and architecture. He described it as a bleak city of concrete construction that lacked the cultural facilities and entertainment centers demanded by modern life. Their absence, he noted, made the place seem "sad and monotonous, as though made sleepful by the somber climate of rain and wind that surrounds it."[35] The dynamic expressiveness of Niemeyer's white sculptural ensemble is accentuated by its setting: surrounding it are Perret's drab, gray, postwar buildings. The latter's pioneering development of reinforced concrete construction provided the foundation for Niemeyer's innovative explorations of the material. More than a case study in applying ferrocon-

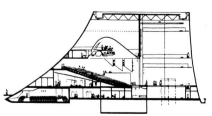

153, 154. Niemeyer,
Maison de la Culture, Le Havre, 1972–82,
theater plan (top) and section through theater (bottom)

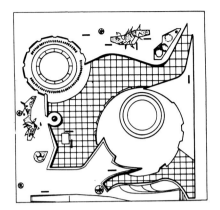

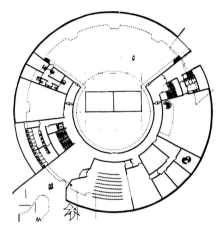

155, 156. Niemeyer,
Maison de la Culture, Le Havre, 1972–82,
site plan (top) and plan of multiuse space (bottom)

crete on an urban scale, Le Havre today splendidly showcases the aesthetic evolution of reinforced concrete architecture.

Niemeyer described his intentions thus:

When I developed this project, my main concern was to integrate it correctly in the architecture of the city. I did not plan, of course, to follow the same type of architecture, which represents a distant epoch, the impositions of that time, and its economics. I wanted my architecture to reveal a new stage in the field of reinforced concrete and to be so simple and abstract that, without being competitive, it accentuated the architectural impact that I imagined.[36]

The program called for a multifunctional complex focused on exhibition spaces and a large theater. The design's double levels and curving composition recall the restaurant and shopping arcade of the Mondadori ensemble, with its recessed plaza open to the sky. Niemeyer described the plaza of Le Havre, sunken three meters below ground to protect it from the port's blustery winds, as a "solution different from all the other squares of Europe." One critic observed that this was "a plaza that dispensed with sculptures because it was in itself a sculpture."[37] The formal emphasis, however, is not on the plaza but on the two sliced conical volumes on either side of it. The first, a hyperboloid, contains administrative offices, exhibition spaces, and audiovisual facilities; the second, a hyperbolic paraboloid, an auditorium with seating for one thousand people, the largest space in the ensemble. Its slight inclination toward one side gives this second volume a remarkable dynamism that recalls the more stable and monumental aesthetic of Le Corbusier's "cooling tower" form in Chandigarh.

While Niemeyer claims that he was not trying to outdo Perret, the formal complexities of the Maison de la Culture seem sufficient evidence that modern Europe's technical domination of the Americas has here been reversed. Niemeyer's forms often speak louder than his rhetoric, and the Le Havre complex is perhaps the most outspoken statement of the Brazilian architect's conquest of Europe—a conquest recognized by the Havrais themselves, who have christened their beloved ensemble "L'Espace Oscar Niemeyer."

Late Works and Archi-Rituals

Niemeyer's major works of the 1980s and 1990s in Brazil demonstrate more clearly than his earlier projects how he has dealt with Brazil's social conflicts. These projects also reveal his attitude toward popular culture and its relationship to his "high" modernism. Niemeyer's architecture has often functioned, sometimes unintentionally, in a process of political co-optation, as a form of populist appeasement and a means to reinforce the social status quo. Through design Niemeyer has sought to wish away the conflicts and dichotomies of Brazilian life by imposing an aesthetic unity that hides the unresolved conflicts by effectively "whitewashing" them. Perhaps most troubling about Niemeyer's architecture is his summary treatment of functional and social differences: his "unified solution" is a wishful refashioning of a reality that remains fundamentally in conflict with his representation of it. This dichotomy is to some extent a function of the Third World context and the realities of a patronage system that continues to demand that the architect innovate for the elite or perish. Impressive public projects that feature formal novelty and monumental scale remain the most powerful means of influencing a largely illiterate and highly impressionable working-class electorate.

One issue continually addressed by Niemeyer's architecture, especially in Brasília and in the last phase of his career, is Brazilian national development—what kind and for whom? While rhetorically championing the cause of the working classes, Niemeyer has continued to accept commissions that have served the status quo and the ruling elite and that have commodified Brazilian culture for consumption by tourists. The commission for the Hotel Nacional in the São Conrado section of Rio's southern zone (1968–72) is a case in point. The Nacional (fig. 158) is the main resort of the Horsa Hotel Company, a family enterprise founded by Brazilian entrepreneur José Tjurs. Horsa was the first national chain to respond to a federal initiative providing fiscal incentives to stimulate tourism. Niemeyer was asked to design a beachfront, high-rise luxury hotel with an adjoining convention center. Touted as the largest hotel in South America when it opened, the Nacional has 510 standard rooms, 27 suites, and capacity for 6,000 convention seats. Its lobby showcases works by important Brazilian artists, including a concrete mural in high relief by Hector Paride Barnabó (also known as Carybé) showing aspects of Brazilian dance and folklore. In the late 1980s a new Horsa management initiated an "incentive travel" program to market Rio, and the São Conrado–Barra de Tijuca area in particular, as a viable destination for North American and European package-deal tourism and the national convention trade.

157. Niemeyer,
Hotel Nacional, Rio de Janeiro, 1968–72

158. Niemeyer,
Hotel Nacional, Rio de Janeiro, 1968–72

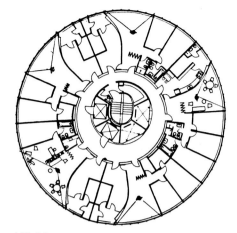

159. Niemeyer,
apartment building for the Barra de Tijuca,
Rio de Janeiro, 1972, sketched plan

The sleek facade of this imposing cylindrical building, with its Miesian black-tinted glass and steel mullions, would seem more at home in a European or North American city than in the tropical fringes of coastal Rio. But for the sophisticated tourist in search of five-star accommodations away from the commotion of Copacabana, the hotel projects a reassuring image of streamlined efficiency, sleek elegance, and metropolitan polish, in a place where such qualities might not be expected. The approach to São Conrado, along the curving Avenida Niemeyer, with its breathtaking view of the ocean below and the *favela* of Vidigal on the hillside above, is dramatic: the black cylinder comes into view as one rounds the curves of the mountain road, only to disappear at the next turn and reappear around the next. Suddenly the structure comes into focus—looming like some monolithic symbol of a cold, technological civilization bent on dominating the virgin forest around it. It stands there hard and erect, an aggressive, masculine presence, imposing itself on the gentle curves of the native landscape like some modern conquistador. More than an ultramodern hotel, the Nacional reads as a symbol of the sexual dominance of the European male over the native female, who is represented by Alfredo Ceschiatti's bronze mermaid sculpture, overlooking the beach from the hotel's poolside deck (fig. 157).

The first large modern structure in the neighborhood, the hotel opened the way for the elite conquest of São Conrado and the Barra de Tijuca, both of which have since become fashionable residential districts. Working within the

160. Niemeyer,
apartment buildings for the Barra de Tijuca,
Rio de Janeiro, 1972, sketch

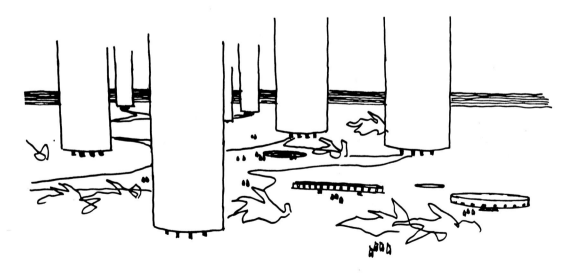

161. Niemeyer,
Hotel Nacional, Rio de Janeiro, 1968–72,
rooftop terrace with core creating a canopy

parameters defined by Lúcio Costa's urbanization scheme for the Barra, during the early 1970s Niemeyer projected seventy-one high-rise condominiums with the same cylindrical form as the hotel (figs. 159, 160). On February 1, 1972, the day the hotel was inaugurated, four condominiums (the Hemingway, the Lincoln, the J. J. Rousseau, and the De Gaulle) opened.[1] As suggested by the names, these Eurocentric projects catered entirely to an international and Brazilian elite and reflected the repressive social context of Brazil's rightist military regime.

The Hotel Nacional is typically *carioca* (and thoroughly Niemeyer) in presenting a facade somewhat at odds with its underlying reality. While its glass-and-steel finish suggests a Miesian steel frame, the structure is actually a concrete core with floors cantilevered outward in a manner reminiscent of Wright's organic skyscraper and the "dendri-form" columns of the Johnson Wax Administration Building. The hotel's structural core mushrooms forth into a circular canopy at the top. Instead of Wright's pine forest, Niemeyer likens the effect to that of an enormous concrete palm tree, a natural metaphor wholly appropriate to the tropical milieu (fig. 161). Unfortunately the potential for an observation balcony beneath the concrete canopy, which commands a breathtaking view of the surrounding coast and mountains, was never exploited: instead cooling units for the air conditioning system were later installed there. This was only one of a number of subsequent alterations to Niemeyer's initial project that later caused the architect to complain that the design had been completely betrayed. He was particularly upset about the positioning of the pool in front of the hotel, which he felt blocked the view of the shore and the sea beyond.[2]

Visibility from within the hotel was foremost in his mind from the start: the rooms are laid out in the circular plan like so many pieces of a pie. The advantage of these wedge-shaped rooms is purely visual—the maximized exterior wall surfaces, glazed from floor to ceiling, provide views of the landscape or seascape beyond. The glass is held in place by continuous vertical metal mullions welded to the exterior. But Niemeyer's search for a scenographic democracy, according to which every room would have an equally splendid view, was betrayed by Brazil's social realities: while some rooms face the sea and the mountains, several look onto Rocinha, a sprawling hillside *favela* that has become a bona fide but brutal neighborhood; home to an estimated 250,000 individuals, it is Latin America's largest permanent shantytown (fig. 162).

162. **The Rocinha *favela*** from the Hotel Nacional

Niemeyer justifies the existence of such *favelas* by condemning the ideology behind their only tried alternative: the mass housing of the modernist mold:

"Workers' housing" and "popular housing" are terms that indicate capitalist discrimination. They represent demagogic and paternalistic objectives that don't attend to the scale of the misery. In fact they aim to prolong the existing situation, to peripheralize the favelados from the most valuable areas, to bury them in these horrible ghettos called conjuntos proletários, or under pretext of security and ecology, to turn the shanty areas to real estate profit.[3]

While there may be some truth to this critique of the diffusionist model, in the absence of a social revolution, Niemeyer's attitude in fact passively reinforces the existence of the *favelas* and the dilemma that produced them.

Niemeyer's approach to social reform through architecture reflects the populist thinking of social scientist Darcy Ribeiro, founder of the University of Brasília.[4] Brazil's development, according to Ribeiro, must be pursued through improving basic educational and cultural facilities, which he promoted in his position as vice governor to the populist governor of the state of Rio de Janeiro, Leonel Brizola. Following in the footsteps of Kubitschek, Brizola and Ribeiro have sought to stimulate large-scale public works in Rio as the means to a new educational and cultural awareness that will foster a greater consciousness of Brazilian identity. The failures of Brasília's social condensers have led Niemeyer too to pursue social reform on a level that he feels is even more basic than housing: that of public education, popular culture, and national ritual.

163. Niemeyer,
Samba Stadium, Rio de Janeiro, 1983–84

In the Samba Stadium (Sambódromo or Passarela do Samba), completed in just four months in 1983 (in time for the Carnaval of 1984), Niemeyer sought to create a unique space and a definitive architectural solution for the yearly celebration of Rio's most popular ritual (figs. 163, 165, 166, 168). Brizola was responsible for the idea of replacing the *arquibancadas* (temporary bleachers of steel tubing) with a more permanent structure that would seat more spectators. He claimed that it cost the public sector $7.5 million each year to subsidize the samba schools and to set up and take down the *arquibancadas*. This amount, he believed, could fund a permanent solution. The initial outlay would be recuperated in a few years, and the money saved and (eventually) earned could be put toward more important social reform projects.[5] A major motivation for the new facility was thus financial, but there remained the problem of justifying such a huge outlay for a permanent complex that would be used only for the several days of Carnaval.

An anteproject for a structure of iron and sheet metal, to be constructed along the major boulevard where the Carnaval parade occurred, had in fact already been approved. However, Brizola, dissatisfied with this solution, decided to consult his specialist in cultural matters, Ribeiro, who suggested approaching his old friend Niemeyer. Niemeyer responded enthusiastically and within four days had submitted five proposals, two for the Avenida Presidente Vargas, the traditional site of the festival, and three for a new site on the Avenida Marquês de Sapucaí, where the most recent parades had been staged. Although Niemeyer initially preferred the first

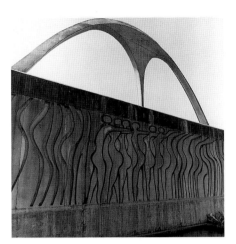

164. Niemeyer,
Samba Stadium, Rio de Janeiro, 1983–84,
arch and sculpture panel (by Marianne Peretti

site in center-city Rio, he soon realized that the boulevard's vital role in the city's circulation system would be seriously compromised by placing the monument in its vicinity: it would not only create chaos for traffic flow but would interfere with the infrastructure beneath the avenue—the subway, electrical systems, water and sewer pipes, and phone cables. The site on the Avenida Marquês de Sapucaí was less congested and could accommodate a space of eighteen thousand square meters, allowing for the creation of what Niemeyer called the Apotheosis Plaza, the development of which was suggested by Ribeiro.

Niemeyer called for the creation of a multifunctional complex that included an open-air cultural center for one hundred thousand spectators with public school classrooms beneath the bleachers. Following the line of thought elaborated by Ribeiro, this creative conflation of national ritual and public instruction was to contribute to the acculturation of Brazilian children, who would learn the pride of being Brazilian and absorb an understanding of the cultural importance of the national ritual. The proposal featured an integrated system of two hundred rooms (forty square meters each) to be used as administrative offices during Carnaval and classrooms during the rest of the year. Twenty billion *cruzeiros* were invested. Sixteen thousand students were to be accommodated in "the biggest school ever built in Brazil." Carnaval thus became, as Niemeyer suggested, "an almost secondary aspect of the Passarela."[6]

The structure is technically daring, with grandstands cantilevered five meters above the ground and suspended boxes that leave a large standing room or general admission area below, open at lower prices. Niemeyer's structural engineer since 1972, Jose Carlos Sussekind, was responsible

165. Niemeyer,
Samba Stadium, Rio de Janeiro, 1983–84,
grandstands and parade ground

for the structural calculations and the extensive use of precast concrete elements in only ten modules. The most daring part of the design, however, is a thin, twenty-five-meter-high arch that supports a concrete slab cantilevered dramatically over the stepped stage at the head of the parade esplanade, crowning the Apotheosis Plaza (figs. 164, 167). The arch's parabolic form—light, graceful, almost ethereal—is a Niemeyer trademark. The back walls of the stage are decorated with Marianne Peretti's abstract representations of Carnaval dancers, and the lateral walls have *azulejo* revetments of curved motifs by Athos Bulcão.

Niemeyer described the ensemble's features thus:

The samba stadium has other functions besides that of the parade pathway itself. It also includes class-rooms for 16,000 students and the large Apotheosis Plaza for music festivals, theater, ballet, and so on. The plans were based on the popular characteristics of the planned events, mainly the carnival parades, which have recently been entirely corrupted. Previously, the people used to watch the parades from the streets, without official limitations or bleachers. It was an event that really belonged to them. Later, the authorities in charge of organizing carnival built bleachers, walling up a narrow pathway of 7 meters width and blocking the people's view of their favorite spectacle. To correct this error, we divided the bleachers into 60-meter blocks and raised them on pilotis, under which people can stand alongside the pathway and see the parade of the samba schools as they did before. And we proposed the inclusion of the Apotheosis Plaza to offer a new aspect to the parade. In terms of its architecture, most important for us was, first of all, to find a simple and functional solution for the unusual integration of the school and bleachers, one that would not compromise its unity. The second step was to give the complex a plastic and innovative sense, something that would mark it as a new symbol of this city. This explains the samba museum, the panel by Marianne Peretti, the azulejos by Athos Bulcão, and the large arch, slim and elegant, free in space, as reinforced concrete permits. And all this gave to the Apotheosis Plaza, monumental with its large space, a new architectonic dimension and that level of good taste and invention inherent in works of art.[7]

166, 167. Niemeyer,
Samba Stadium, Rio de Janeiro, 1983–84,
grandstands and parade ground (top) and
arch in Apotheosis Plaza (bottom)

168. Niemeyer,
Samba Stadium, Rio de Janeiro, 1983–84,
grandstands and parade ground

Ribeiro emphasized that the monument would become a "a new symbol of *carioca* civilization," and he compared it to the old colonial aqueduct of Lapa, the Maracanã stadium, and Corcovado and Sugar Loaf mountains. He also called attention to the importance of collaboration in achieving the desired goals:

We managed to make public administration sufficiently flexible and efficient to allow our national engineering to achieve such a feat and our educators to create a new democratic model for public schools. The Parade avenue complex is today the cultural space in which cariocas are free to re-identify themselves as the happy, free, and creative people that we are, with the courage to think, create, perform, and joke—things that register our existence in this world [fig. 169].

The complex's structural engineer, Sussekind, presented the stadium as a masterwork of national engineering: "Once again, Brazilian engineering set a new record for its annals: 17 thousand cubic meters of reinforced concrete were produced and 85 thousand square meters built in 120 days, right on schedule."[8]

For all of this, the project has been criticized for repeating the defects of the temporary bleachers: poor visibility, no protection from rain, difficult rest-room access, crowding all of the samba schools into one space at the head of the parade avenue. Tickets to see the parade are now more expensive and harder to get, especially for the box seats with the privileged view from above. In 1988, there was a 700 percent increase in the price of tickets, the cheapest ones selling for forty dollars, about the equivalent of a monthly salary for Rio's poorest workers. They are now forced to watch the event on television. Fortunately, the lighting and visibility for television have been markedly improved in the stadium.[9] The commodification and commercialization of Carnaval as a prepackaged product to be consumed by tourists has thus been well served by the complex. Some ill-informed observers have gone so far as to suggest that the great arch in the Apotheosis Plaza is Niemeyer's stylization of McDonald's "golden arches." Nothing could be further from the intentions of an architect who sees North American capitalism as the source of all evil. Still others, more observant, have seen in the arch's contours the ubiquitous *bum-bum* with the "dental floss" bikini of the female samba dancers, a much more likely source, given Niemeyer's interest in female form. For his part, Niemeyer casts the project as a "second Brasília," of national pride and import, completed in record

169. **Samba Stadium** with Carnaval floats and performers

time—yet another ritual performance of Brazilian modernism.[10]

The Samba Stadium reflects the effort to structure the Carnaval ritual in such a way that it becomes the centerpiece of a new sense of popular participation in Brazilian culture and a new symbol of national identity. Its construction on the working-class outskirts of downtown Rio, however, suggests a certain marginalization of the event and its participants, as if the (European) business district could no longer handle the "messiness" of an Afro-Brazilian ritual. Traditionally, Carnaval has inverted normal class relations: the *povão* (popular class) becomes "king of the city" for the duration of the celebration. Fixing the Carnaval parade in an architectural context outside the city center implies a demagogic, elitist restructuring of popular ritual that more clearly distinguishes participants and observers, performers and consumers, "us" and "them."

Niemeyer's solution is one that seems to be at fundamental odds with the libertine spirit of Carnaval: the spaces and structures of the stadium effectively "invert the inversions" of the normally fluid ritual through their concern with an orderly spatial procession with a clearly defined beginning and end and clearly defined participants and spectators. The ritual process now seems less important than the pragmatic ends: the judging of the winning samba school, the media image, the making of money for "the state." Reinforcing these criticisms is the fact that the traditional Carnaval decorations were banned from display in the building in 1984, when it was inaugurated, only to be reinstated in 1988. Many people feel that without these decorations, the stadium is a lifeless concrete forest. But Niemeyer and Ribeiro disagree: they find the decorations an abomination that disrespects Niemeyer's work and that, in effect, sullies his unified solution.[11] The effort of Niemeyer and his patrons to sanitize the messiness and diversity of Carnaval and control the arbitrary chaos that is central to the ritual seems at odds with the rhetoric of "a Carnaval that belongs to the people." Niemeyer and his patrons here demonstrate their mastery of the fine art of social engineering. This is perhaps the strongest link between the Samba Stadium and Brasília: expensive projects that purport to give something truly Brazilian back to the people in fact not so subtly take it away.

Niemeyer and the Centros Integrados de Educação Pública The social and cultural program of the Samba Stadium should be seen in the context of the development of the Centros Integrados de Educação Pública (CIEPs; 1983–84), another highly controversial undertaking sponsored by Brizola, inspired by Ribeiro, and given architectural expression by Niemeyer (figs. 170, 171).[12] The project was

170. Niemeyer,
Centro Integrado de Educação Pública,
Catete, Rio de Janeiro, 1983–84

intended to address a basic problem in the state of Rio de Janeiro: illiteracy and the lack of educational facilities for impoverished children. Conceived by Ribeiro and Brizola as a model that could be implemented nationwide, the CIEPs, or *Brizolões* as they are popularly known, sought to guarantee classroom space for the state's school-age children who were not served by the public system. (At the start of 1983, this number was seven hundred thousand.) Ribeiro envisioned the CIEPs as an educational revolution that would radically change the social panorama of a state in which 52 percent of the students never finished second grade. Each center was to accommodate one thousand full-time students, with twenty classrooms, a library, medical and dental clinics, a gymnasium, and a cafeteria. Niemeyer proposed a standardized design using precast modular elements in reinforced concrete; such a system, he argued, would be faster and, compared to conventional brick construction, 30-percent cheaper to build. Nonetheless, conservative estimates placed the cost for each unit at $1.3 million.[13] Brizola wanted to erect five hundred such centers throughout the state, concentrating on the areas in and around the city of Rio where they were most needed. By the end of his administration in 1987, 127 CIEPs had been completed, 112 of which were functioning. Another 47 were in the final phases of construction, and 105 others were being built.[14]

The CIEPs have been criticized for leaky roofs and high maintenance costs, which, according to the state, are almost twice that for conventional school structures. Teachers and students have complained about the noise level in the classrooms, a problem exacerbated by wall partitions that do not reach the ceiling. More basic was the criticism that the cost per child was too high and that Rio's other public schools were being neglected in order to provide "social assistance" for *favelados*. Blaming a lack of funds, Brizola's successor, Moreira Franco, discontinued the project, leaving the skeletons and construction modules of the unfinished CIEPs in a state of wasteful abandon. The *carioca* press, critical of the project from the start, and especially of the political dividends sought by its populist patrons (Ribeiro, for example, had his eye on a senate seat), began to refer to the sites as "CIEP cemeteries."[15] In March 1990, the Rio daily *O Globo* reported that many of the abandoned buildings had been taken over by homeless and unemployed people who installed their families in the classrooms and refused to leave.[16] In 1991, Brizola, recently reelected governor, resumed sponsorship of the project, taking his proposals directly to the president of the Republic, Fernando Collor, who agreed to fund the construction of five thousand new CIEPs

171 Niemeyer,
Centro Integrado de Educação Pública,
Catete, Rio de Janeiro, 1983–84, main facade

throughout the country at a total cost of $1.2 billion. Niemeyer, not a supporter of the administration's right-of-center politics, was replaced by a new team of architects: João Filgueiras Lima and the structural engineer Sussekind, whose proposals for the new units called for a pyramidal structure that would accommodate seven hundred students and cost far less than Niemeyer's scheme—$240,000.[17] Collor's programs, however, were severely compromised by a corruption scandal that forced him to resign from office in December 1992.

Monumento Tortura Nunca Mais and Monumento Volta Redonda in Rio de Janeiro

Niemeyer graphically expressed his revolt against the atrocities of Brazil's military regime in an unexecuted project commissioned in 1986 by the group Tortura Nunca Mais (Torture Never Again). The monument was to pay tribute to the thousands of persecuted Brazilians who were tortured, abducted, or detained by the military between the coup of April 1964 and the end of the dictatorship in March 1985. From the testimony of 1,843 political prisoners, researchers of human rights violations in Brazil have documented the existence between 1964 and 1979 of 444 torturers using 283 different types of torture in 242 clandestine centers; 125 political prisoners were reported to have disappeared.[18] In October 1986 an exhibition featuring the works of Brazil's major artists was organized to raise money for the monument, which would have been inconceivable before the advent in 1985 of the democratically elected government. Niemeyer sought to dramatize the shocking violence and horror of the theme: he proposed a huge concrete arc, twenty-five meters long and seven meters tall, elevated on a rectangular platform reached via an internal staircase. Dangling at the end of the arc would be a life-size human figure, its body brutally impaled by the projectile. Niemeyer thus created an image of terror that weighs heavy, physically and spiritually, on the eye and conscience of the observer. The proposed site in Rio's Gloria-Flamengo park, Burle Marx's masterpiece of urban landscaping, resulted in a bitter diatribe between the architect and the landscape designer in the local press.[19] The monument was never erected.

In the Monumento Volta Redonda (Memorial Nove de Novembro) Niemeyer extended his artistic protest to address the plight of the exploited working classes. On November 9, 1988, a peaceful steel workers' strike in Volta Redonda (150 kilometers from Rio) tragically escalated when the military police killed three workers. Niemeyer paid tribute to the three in a highly polemical monument inaugurated in Rio on May 1, 1989. A large wall, arched over at the top and roughly resembling half of a barrel vault, featured abstracted figures of the three men. The central figure was pierced by a huge

172. Niemeyer,
Memorial da América Latina, São Paulo,
1989, with *Bleeding Hand* and suspended
pedestrian bridge

concrete arrow that entered the sculpture from the side at a dramatically oblique angle. Red paint beneath the figures represented the flow of blood from their bodies into a larger pool at the base.

In the early morning hours of the day following the inauguration, the monument was dynamited by a right-wing neo-Nazi faction of the Brazilian military called the National Patriotic Front. In the wake of the outrage following the sabotage, Niemeyer vowed to reconstruct the monument, despite unidentified threats that it would be blown up yet again. Niemeyer countered this with a design for a smaller concrete monument showing the bomb marks of the sabotage but eliminating the pool of blood. He warned that "not even acts of terrorism would force those who fight for democracy to keep quiet." Because no construction firm willing to risk involvement in the new project could be found, the steel workers themselves erected the monument, which was inaugurated on August 12, 1989. At its base Niemeyer installed a bronze plaque with his own words: "Nothing, not even the bomb that destroyed the Memorial, can stop those who fight for liberty and social justice."[20]

The Tortura Nunca Mais and Volta Redonda monuments illustrate Niemeyer's increasing interest in the use of a new, politically charged sculptural expression. The style is brutal and direct, the

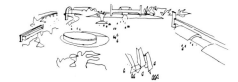

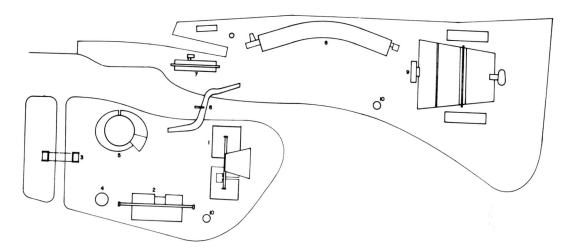

173, 174. Niemeyer,
Memorial da América Latina, São Paulo,
1989, sketch (top) and plan (bottom)

political content overt. The intensity of these works no doubt reflects the long years of

repression and personal frustration that the architect experienced during the military

regime. As an architect and political polemicist, Niemeyer is most powerful when

given the freedom to focus on a work's sculptural and symbolic essence.

The Memorial da América Latina in São Paulo The expressive integration of architecture and

sculpture, of biomorphic form and symbolic content, is Niemeyer's most characteristic achievement. When

this synthesis occurs within the framework of monumental projects that answer to the utopian impulse preva-

lent in his work, the result is a powerful multimedia experience such as that offered by the Memorial da

América Latina in São Paulo (1989; figs. 172–74). While its biomorphic free forms and daring structures

grow out of formal innovations developed over his long career, the explicit political content of the monu-

ments should be seen in the context of his recent protest monuments. The Memorial da América Latina is

175. Niemeyer,
Memorial da América Latina, São Paulo,
1989, with suspended pedestrian bridge (left) and
Salão de Atos (right)

the crowning achievement of Niemeyer's career: a masterful ensemble that displays

the surrealist tendency and sculptural intensity of a master at the height of his creative

power. The memorial is a carnival of past achievements brought together on a new

stage and in a new space for the imagination.

The memorial is Niemeyer's most grandiose and ambitious ritual

gesture since Brasília; its goal is nothing less than the creation and expression of a

new sense of Latin American cultural unity. A monumental collaborative venture spon-

sored by the government of the state of São Paulo, the memorial illustrates how

176. Niemeyer,
Administration building and Brazilian Center for Latin American Studies,
Memorial da América Latina, São Paulo, 1989

177. Niemeyer,
Salão de Atos, Memorial da América Latina, São Paulo, 1989

178. Niemeyer,
Latin American Parliament Building,
Memorial da América Latina, São Paulo, 1989–92

Niemeyer has attempted to give harmonious, abstract form to a project motivated by several different visions of a better society for Brazil and Latin America. For Niemeyer and his patron, São Paulo's governor, Orestes Quércia, the memorial's official purpose is to give concrete expression to Latin American integration and thus initiate that ambitious project.

The flowing layout recalls Niemeyer's 1962 project for the International Exposition Complex in Tripoli. The site, divided by a multilane avenue, consists of two amorphous concrete compounds connected by a suspended, curving ramp-bridge for pedestrians (fig. 175). The complex has six major functional units housed in separate pavilions, recalling exposition architecture: the Salão de Atos, a ceremonial hall for official gatherings and a collection of commemorative art (figs. 177, 179); the first public library in South America devoted exclusively to Latin American cultures (figs. 180, 185); the Pavilhão de Criatividade (Creativity Pavilion), containing permanent exhibits focusing on the craft production of Latin America's indigenous cultures; the Aula Magna, a two-thousand-seat auditorium for musical and theatrical presentations, congresses, and other cultural events (figs. 182–84); the Brazilian Center for Latin American Studies, with scholarships, exchange, and monthly seminar programs (fig. 176); and the Latin American Parliament Building, recently erected in front of the Pavilhão de Criatividade and not part of the original project (fig. 178).

179. Niemeyer,
Salão de Atos, Memorial da América Latina, São Paulo, 1989, plan

180. Niemeyer,
Library, Memorial da América Latina, São Paulo, 1989, plan

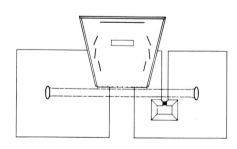

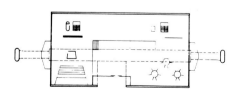

The memorial's program of cultural unity came from Ribeiro, who laments Latin America's political fragmentation and especially Brazil's historical isolation from its South American neighbors. Building the complex in São Paulo, Brazil's largest and wealthiest city (and the third-largest city in the world), is a gesture to the rest of Latin America, signifying São Paulo's and Brazil's desire both to lead the project and to participate in the community. The memorial is to provide a spatio-cultural forum, a central meeting place for all Latin American peoples, and a means to raise Brazilian and especially São Paulo consciences about Spanish and indigenous American cultures and what it means to be Latin American.

The ambitious project of cultural consciousness-raising is reflected in the architectural forms of the library and the Salão de Atos. Both structures are framed by tall twin pillars, abstract and monumental, that rise up majestically like the bell towers of a great baroque church. In addition to providing a visual link with the verticality of the skyscrapers in the cityscape beyond, integrating the ensemble's hori-

181. Niemeyer,
Bleeding Hand, Memorial da América Latina,
São Paulo, 1989, ink and watercolor drawing

zontal forms into the urban context, these towers function structurally—to anchor and carry the horizontal beams supporting the roofs—and symbolically—to create a ritual gravity and religious solemnity. Open to the public every day, the Salão is intended to be "the most solemn space in São Paulo as well as the most popular."[21] It showcases several important works by Brazilian artists that foster reverence for the culture, history, and important figures of Latin America. Children are to "feel enraptured" by Candido Portinari's mural depicting the martyrdom of the leader of Brazil's thwarted national liberation movement, Tiradentes, and by the sculptural panels in low relief by Carybé and Napoleon Potyguara Lazzaroto (Poty), which portray the ethnic diversity of Latin America's native and immigrant peoples. Spiritually moved to heightened cultural awareness by such images, the public may pursue the deeper meanings of these artistic object lessons in Latin American history in the library. The library and Salão de Atos are thus modern cathedrals to Latin American culture and learning that seek to stimulate a new popular ritual—the contemplation (and analysis) of Latin diversity, liberation, and suffering—and to celebrate a new mass: a Latin America unified by shared experiences.

Ribeiro calls attention to the mythic-religious associations and ritual significance of the memorial by comparing it to Aleijadinho's baroque Terrace of the Prophets in Congonhas do Campo. The memorial, like the sanctuary, "will remain untouched, through the passage of time, bearing witness to the creativity and dignity of our own generation. . . . It will attract all those pilgrims who search to cleanse their eyes in beauty, that magic, miraculous ingredient so necessary to human beings, as there are so few who do not feel some type of hunger for beauty."

182. Niemeyer,
Aula Magna, Memorial da América Latina,
São Paulo, 1989, upper floor plan

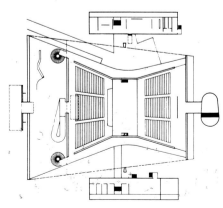

Informing the basic conception is the shared memory of a characteristically Latin, baroque aesthetic unity conducive to the spiritual quest for eternity and redemption. Ribeiro and Niemeyer see the integration of all arts in a multimedia ensemble as a metaphor for the integration of Latin American cultures. Perhaps the clearest visual expression of the utopian theme is Bruno Giorgi's abstract marble sculpture *Integração*, composed of two inverted forms interlocking to create one. Regional diversity is expressed as well: live concerts by Latin American musicians and a restaurant specializing in the region's cuisine add to the total immersion of the senses in Latin American culture.

Beneath the official agenda of integration are several others: The

183. Niemeyer,
Aula Magna, Memorial da América Latina,
São Paulo, 1989

184. Niemeyer,
Library, Memorial da América Latina,
São Paulo, 1989

memorial is part of a long tradition of great works sponsored by ambitious politicians seeking to leave their marks on history by bequeathing to society monuments of great import and popular appeal. The memorial emerges as that typically Brazilian ritual of political, economic, intellectual, and artistic collaboration in which a small group creates a landmark architectural development in record time, in this case seventeen months. The memorial has thus been compared to Niemeyer's other successful monumental collaborations. As Ribeiro notes, "by creating the Memorial, governor Orestes Quércia repeats [ex-president] Juscelino Kubitschek's historic position that revolutionized Brazilian architecture in the 1940s, when he chose Oscar to build Pampulha." More importantly, he says, the memorial "will represent an architectural compound equivalent in its magnitude only to Brasília." Quércia, who aspired to Brazil's presidency, claims to have dreamed of the memorial as a gubernatorial candidate, just as Kubitschek during his presidential campaign appealed to the popular idea of constructing a new capital for Brazil. For his part, Ribeiro situates the "Memorial Oscárico" alongside his own recent collaborative projects with Niemeyer: the Samba Stadium and the CIEPs in Rio de Janeiro. These too were projects that sought to promote national culture and effect far-reaching reforms in Brazilian society.

The interests of capitalist developers in São Paulo have also been an important impetus for the memorial project. Brazil's industrial elite, especially several major construction and engineering firms, materials suppliers, and manufacturers of decorative design products see the project as an opportunity to market their enterprises throughout the continent. The São Paulo Metropolitan Subway Corporation, which has provided major funding for the undertaking, views the project not in terms of Latin American community, but as a means to expand São Paulo's transportation infrastructure and stimulate public use of mass transit. The site is adjacent to the new, futurist Barra Funda subway station, which the subway company would like to see emerge as a main transport and commercial hub for central São Paulo. Meanwhile, the minister of Housing and Urban Development considers the project a convenient means to revitalize a run-down industrial district that was on the verge of being overtaken by shanties. A new shopping mall is planned.

Added to these special interests is Ribeiro and Niemeyer's desire to express the ideals of Latin American unity and the Marxist dream of social justice. Inherent contradictions spring from the conflicts among Brazilian nationalist goals, the ambitions and capitalist interests of wealthy São Paulo, and the dream of Latin American integration. Ribeiro himself expresses a certain ambivalence in this respect: "This magnificent Oscárić ensemble, coupled with the ambitious cultural program, will make São

Paulo into one of the cultural capitals of Latin America, giving Brazilians a nucleus around which to intensify solidarity amongst our people and cultivate a critical conscience of our reality and potential." Here he seems to refer to Brazilian and especially São Paulo realities and potentials, but he catches himself and quickly adds: "The Brazilian Center for Latin American Studies, the motor of the Memorial, faithful to the ideals of Bolívar, has nevertheless the fundamental objective of contributing to the creation of a Latin American nation, with a regional common market and a Latin American Parliament." It remains to be seen how the conflicting forces of nationalism, capitalism, continental integration, and social justice for the masses will be resolved by the memorial.

Finally, Niemeyer's own aesthetic project was the obstinate search for a visual utopia: he hoped to transcend politics (almost) entirely by creating an inspiring work of beautiful art that would, through its great unity and monumentality, elevate (if only momentarily) the humanity that beheld it out of the dismal grind of urban existence in modern-day São Paulo. Niemeyer's ensemble attempts to resolve the conflicts and contradictions of the integration project artistically, through an uncompromising abstraction within which freedom and unity, the twin pillars of this utopia, coexist harmoniously on the aesthetic level. The free-form layout and the formal diversity of the pavilions, unified by the opposition of flat black glass and curving white concrete, illustrate this effort.

In designing the complex Niemeyer sought to create a monumental "architectural spectacle" that would reflect its serious theme. The complex is to be experienced by commuters who, emerging from the depths of the subway station via a staircase that leads into the ensemble, would "be inspired by the enormous impact of this architectural wonder": "While designing the Memorial, my greatest concern was to make it so different, so free and creative, imbued with such plastic unity that it would incite, right from the start, the astonishment every work of art must inspire."[22] Niemeyer created an element of surprise and marvel through daring structural acrobatics typified by his "free-in-the-air" pedestrian bridge and the suspended Brazilian Center for Latin American Studies, which recalls his own Museum of the City of Brasília.

Such structural magic and the myth of the genius are of course typical of Niemeyer and the modernist utopian project: echoing Lúcio Costa's method in designing the winning plan for Brasília, Niemeyer describes how his inspired perspective for the memorial complex came to him spontaneously "as if a premonition had suddenly taken hold."[23] The progression of spaces and visual experience of the architectural and sculptural objects in this Corbusian *promenade architecturale* appear, however, to

185. Niemeyer,
Library, Memorial da América Latina,
São Paulo, 1989

186. Niemeyer,
Bleeding Hand, Memorial da América Latina,
São Paulo, 1989

have been carefully resolved. Sensitive to the powerful motivating force of basic human impulses—hunger, thirst, spending money—he placed the restaurant directly adjacent to the stairway from which weary commuters emerge. This delicious solution of course increases the likelihood that this potentially lucrative aspect of the memorial's "cultural program" will be well patronized.

Once out of the snack bar, however, it is practically impossible to approach the Salão de Atos, the ritual center of the complex, without passing by and coming to terms with what Niemeyer intended to be the sculptural centerpiece of the complex: his dramatic "gesture of human solidarity" is the seven-meter-tall *Bleeding Hand* in reinforced concrete (figs. 181, 186) that recalls Le Corbusier's Monument to the Open Hand at Chandigarh. More than a tribute to his European mentor and an appropriate summation of the Brazilian's fundamental artistic debt, Niemeyer's open hand also expresses the frustrations of a continent exploited by Western imperialism. For here is depicted what Eduardo Galeano calls the "open veins of Latin America":[24] a hand spread out, with desperately splayed fingers, a stigmata with a map of Latin America trickling sacrificial blood down the wrist—a hand whose form says "Chega! Basta! Enough exploitation!" At Governor Quércia's insistence, Niemeyer toned down the political invective of the inscription that was to be placed on the base of the hand. Later the architect wrote, "This is a hand that reminds us of past days of strife, poverty, and abandonment." Mindful that that past is still present for many, he added: "Life is full of sorrow and happiness—'twin sisters'—as Jorge Luis Borges called them, but we must never forget that, long before him, old Marx said we ourselves must change it."[25] If socioeconomic integration is the dream for the future of Latin America, Niemeyer's *Bleeding Hand* recalls the serious inequalities of the past and present that must be overcome to make that dream come true. It also questions the viability of a capitalist model of integration. A Marxist call to arms in a monument patronized by state capitalism and wealthy patrons? This is typical Niemeyer.

So is the dialogue that he maintains with his "other" self, his "twin brother"—to borrow (and transform) Borges's phrase—over the conflict between social responsibility and monumental architecture. Fully aware that the memorial represents a model of social integration molded by the Brazilian elite, of which he is an ambivalent part, Niemeyer explains apologetically:

I have done very few projects of a social nature, and I must admit that whenever I do one, I feel like I'm conniving with the demagogic and paternalistic objective they stand for, fooling the working class that demands higher wages and the advantage of having better opportunities. . . . On the other hand, I never felt afraid of monumentality when the theme in itself demanded it. After all, what remained of architecture over the ages were the monumental works, those that represent the evolution of techniques—those which, fair or unfair from the social point of view, still manage to move us. Beauty imposes itself on the sensibility of men.[26]

As he concluded long ago, when designing Brasília, "It is strange how the power of beauty makes us forget so much injustice."[27]

The function of Niemeyer's art, then, is to create an aesthetic utopia that visually nourishes the Latin American spirit and thus enables it to put up with the harsh day-to-day reality that the architect cannot change. At the same time, Niemeyer shuns art as social escapism by inserting into his utopian ensembles politically charged elements like *Bleeding Hand*, brutal elements that shock through contrast and thus suggest the flip side of the beauty: the injustice, the lost Communist alternative, and the anger that Niemeyer and many Latin Americans feel about the failed utopia that was to bring more just social development to the region's peoples.

So the memorial is a study in contrasting but inseparable "twins": black and white; ugly industrial city and beautiful utopian ensemble; the monumental and the socially responsible; forgetfulness and the remembrance of things past (and present); the abstract and the detailed; the general and the specific; sorrow and happiness; rich and poor; Marxist rhetoric and capitalist reality; Brazilian and Latin American. What unifies these twins is their status *as* twins; what brings unity to the free forms of Niemeyer's pavilions and to the diversity of peoples in Latin America is the shared experience, or at least perception, of extreme contrasts. Niemeyer's abstract resolution, really his whitewashing of this dialectic itinerary, lends his work to a wide variety of different causes and interests. The vague visual rhetoric of abstract formalism is the key: no room for details here, just pure and sensual form, he emphasizes.

One of the details that the ensemble seeks to obscure is its own ideology, which is ultimately elitist and demagogic, even in relation to the Latin American culture that it proposes to champion. Hidden beneath Niemeyer's white unity is a clear distinction between the high modernism of the Brazilians, which unifies (i.e., controls) the complex, and the craft art of the rest of Latin America, which is put on display in the Pavilhão de Criatividade and thus effectively commodified. The memorial highlights the abstract modernist contributions of Niemeyer, Portinari, and other Brazilian artists at the expense of the other cultures of Latin America (especially the native Indian and African contributions), which are presented as token artifacts of a distant past, now forced into museum format by the French curators. The primacy of

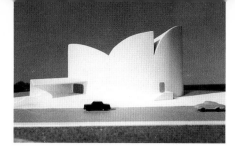

187. Niemeyer,
Araras Theater, 1991, model

the Brazilian modernist contribution implies a model of integration controlled by a Eurocentric elite.

The memorial's abstract unity is rooted in an inability or unwillingness to come to terms with its own uncompromising polarities, rooted as these are in the profound socioeconomic inequalities of Latin American experience. Instead this high art projects a lofty utopian vision—a grandiose conception of Latin American culture—that patronizes the masses, who once again are forced to accept their condition and the absence of details concerning a more acceptable middle ground of real reform and improvement. The memorial thus illustrates the role that Niemeyer's modernism has played in popular co-optation—to borrow Youssef Cohen's phrase once again, "the manipulation of consent."

Niemeyer has often been criticized for his insensitivity to the details of human use. The memorial has been attacked as a cold and unwelcoming place, yet another example of concrete monotony that could have been relieved by a tropical garden by Burle Marx. There are few places to sit and no shade except that provided by the buildings' long shadows. On a typical summer's day, the heat and near blinding light of the tropical sun reflected off the burning concrete force one to seek refuge in one of the pavilions, where the environment is at least cooler if no more inviting. Nor has the planting of palm trees alongside the new parliament building done much to change this situation. Despite the openness of the space, the compound can have the closed feeling of a military precinct: tall fences and security gates make it difficult for the person on the street to enter. Like the Samba Stadium, the compound comes alive only when filled with people.

For all of its shortcomings, the memorial illustrates not only the refinement of Niemeyer's structural and compositional techniques, but the maturation of his late style into a surrealistically expressive art that reflects the persistence of his approach to architecture—the effort to resolve (or wish away) the contradictions of realities in a harmonious visual synthesis that, like an expensive Carnaval costume, elegantly masks the unresolved conflicts underneath. As in Carnaval, the basis of Niemeyer's unity and ritual is the inversion itself. At eighty-six, Niemeyer has become an enduring Latin American tradition perhaps entitled to one last great ritual of utopian modernism, with all of its inherent contradictions. Yet Niemeyer himself does not yet seem to realize that the shock of his "new" now seems quite old, and not nearly as shocking as it was thirty years ago.

The Araras Theater Niemeyer's association with Governor Quércia led to another controversial project that reveals the extent of governmental corruption in Brazil and brings into question the seriousness of the two men's commitment to social justice. In 1991, Quércia's mother-in-law requested that he obtain funds from the state Ministry of Culture to pay for a new theater to be erected in his wife Alaíde's home-town, Araras, a small city 170 kilometers from São Paulo. Quércia promptly secured a project from Niemeyer (fig. 187) and responded flatly to inquiries from the press: "A mother-in-law's request cannot be refused."[28] The press, calling the project the "Teatro da Sogra" (Mother-in-Law's Theater), responded with outrage. An unidentified columnist wrote:

At a moment when the state is almost bankrupt, with its coffers emptied by election expenses; at a moment when practically all public works have been paralyzed and the civil servants are going through the bitter situation . . . of receiving their salaries late—in Araras, in the interior of São Paulo state, a supermodern theater—in an eleven-story building for 466 spectators, designed by Oscar Niemeyer—is being construct-ed in the record time of six months. A bold and polemical undertaking, in the form of an immense cylinder costing $5 million and on which are working 360 laborers of a Bahian construction firm, in two alternat-ing teams, twenty-four hours a day and seven days a week. . . . The fact that a theater of this grandeur is being constructed with public money in a city with only one cinema and one daily showtime is already a sufficient theme for the "theater of the absurd." But when we realize that not far from this white elephant in the making, there is a construction site for a future hospital that has been practically paralyzed, . . . the subject is no longer comic, but becomes instead quite tragic.[29]

Another commentator pointed out that the money spent on the theater could have been used for badly needed low-cost housing for the city, which has a population of only around one hundred thousand and no local theater group. As the local secretary of culture conceded: "It's going to be difficult to fill the theater."[30] As for Niemeyer, his position seems clear enough: "I am an architect who works for whoever calls me."[31]

The Museu de Arte Contemporânea in Niterói Niemeyer's most recent major undertakings reflect a reworking of favorite themes from his own unexecuted projects of the past. The most compelling of these new monuments is the Museu de Arte Contemporânea in Niterói (1991; fig. 188). The creation of the $5-million museum is part of an urban "face-lift" campaign sponsored by the municipality of Niterói, and especially by its mayor, Jorge Roberto Silveira, and his secretary of culture, Italo Campofiorito, to give the

188. Niemeyer,
Museu de Arte Contemporânea, Niterói,
1991, under construction

city a new image and turn it into a cultural center that will attract local and international tourism. Just across the bay from Rio and accessible via ferry and a monumental highway bridge, Niterói has long suffered from an inferiority complex because of its traditional dormitory status in relation to Rio. As a popular saying has it, "The best thing about Niterói is the view of Rio." Niemeyer's design and the dramatic siting of the museum suggest that he would not disagree. Perched high on a picturesque promontory above the Praia de Boa Viagem and commanding a splendid panoramic view of Sugar Loaf and Corcovado mountains, the museum is in the form of a chalice, a suavely curved reworking of the inverted pyramidal form of the unexecuted Museu de Arte Moderna for Caracas. The Niterói museum is a piece of pure science fiction turned real—for Niemeyer, a form long dreamt of finally come true. The building's saucer-shaped main volume, housing the exhibition space, hovers above its site like a UFO about to land on earth, bringing with it the material evidence of some advanced civilization intent on enlightening the culturally inferior earthlings of Niterói. The sophisticated objects in question are the roughly fifteen hundred abstract artworks in the collection of João Leão Sattamini (one of the largest holders of Brazilian contemporary art), which will be permanently displayed in the building. The museum, it is hoped, will become one of the state's most important cultural points.

Both the Memorial da América Latina and the Niterói museum have been criticized as yet two more instances of the favoritism shown Niemeyer by government patrons: neither commission was awarded through an open competition. The museum, however, speaks of more than Niemeyer's conquest of government patronage and the attempted modernist conquest of reinforced concrete, visionary space, and mass culture: it is also Niemeyer's most eloquent statement to date about the redemptive role of art in a society that he believes he cannot change. Niemeyer's concrete chalice of redemption contains not the eucharistic wine symbolizing the blood of Christ but the sacramental objects of a different, modernist communion. Nothing could be more characteristic than this outspoken expression of continuing faith in the sacred power of abstract art to lift humankind out of its dismal material existence and into a nebulous spiritual realm as otherworldly as this spaceship-chalice. The museum is thus above all a synthesizing and symbolic statement, a formal conflation of Christian and modernist utopian imagery that has become the essence of Niemeyer's formal ritualization of high modernism.

Ultimately, however, Niemeyer's real redemption is personal rather than social and lies in his return to the biomorphic forms of the Brazilian landscape. This is clear in his project for an exposition annex for Ibirapuera Park in São Paulo (fig. 189), first displayed at the 1993 architecture biennial held there. Here Niemeyer comes full circle, for the form recalls his early unexecuted project for the theater with twin auditoriums adjoining the Ministry of Education and Health Building in Rio. The work's ultimate source—the seductive curves of Rio's mountains, waves, and women—will continue to inspire Niemeyer's most deeply felt and dialectically charged architecture. For in this case, it is not so much the contents of the new exposition hall that matter (more abstract art) as its curving and suggestive external form. In the end, Niemeyer confesses, "Woman is the most important of all."[32]

The important challenge of going beyond attractive appearances and imagining functions genuinely appropriate to the formidable problems of a developing nation continues to take a backseat to creating seductive forms that express the elitist status quo in a way that masks its inequalities or makes them seem acceptable. Niemeyer's aesthetic resolution—his heavy-handed way of dealing with differences—remains forced, the Brazilian dilemma unresolved. Beyond the forms, the greatest success of Niemeyer's architecture is clearly that it has most often not only reflected but even reinforced the basic dilemmas that continue to characterize Brazilian society. As Miguel Alves Pereira, Ferreira Gullar, and other critics have long since concluded, Niemeyer is largely responsible for the persistence of the idea that the only way out of the Brazilian dilemma, as long as the problem of underdevelopment remains, is to continue producing an architecture focused primarily on plastic values and formal innovations.[33] It is an idea, they believe, that most Brazilians have yet to question.

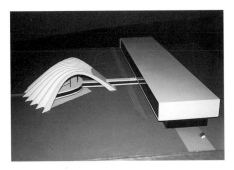

189. Niemeyer,
**project for exposition annex at Ibirapuera
Park,** São Paulo, 1993, model

Major Works and Projects

The years in the headings refer to initial project dates. Years the buildings were actually begun are indicated where necessary; years of completion, if different, are noted in parentheses. Unexecuted designs are listed as projects.

1936
Project for Henrique Xavier House, Rio de Janeiro.

Project for University City, Rio de Janeiro (with Lúcio Costa, Carlos Leão, Affonso Reidy, and others, under the direction of Le Corbusier).

Ministry of Education and Health Building, Rio de Janeiro (with Lúcio Costa, Carlos Leão, Affonso Reidy, Jorge Moreira, and Ernani Vasconcelos, under the direction of Le Corbusier), begun 1937 (1943).

1937
Obra do Berço (Day Nursery), Rio de Janeiro (1940). Engineer: Emilio Baumgarten.

1938
Weekend House for Oswaldo de Andrade, São Paulo.

Brazilian Pavilion for New York World's Fair, New York (with Lúcio Costa and Paul Lester Wiener) (1939), destroyed.

Grand Hotel, Ouro Prêto, Minas Gerais (1940). Engineer: Albino Froufe.

1939
Project for Weekend House for M. Passos, Miguel Pereira, Rio de Janeiro.

1940
Casino at Pampulha, Minas Gerais (today Museum of Fine Arts) (1942). Engineer: Joaquim Cardozo.

Casa do Baile (Restaurant and Dance Hall), Pampulha, Minas Gerais (1942). Engineer: Albino Froufe.

Yacht Club, Pampulha, Minas Gerais (1942). Engineer: Joaquim Cardozo.

Chapel of São Francisco de Assis, Pampulha, Minas Gerais, begun 1943 (1944). Engineer: Joaquim Cardozo.

Brazilian Industry Exhibition, Buenos Aires, Argentina.

1941
Project for Water Tower, Ribeiro das Lages, Rio de Janeiro.

Project for National Sports Center and Stadium, Rio de Janeiro.

1942
Niemeyer House (Lagoa House), near the Lagoa Rodrigo de Freitas, Rio de Janeiro.

1943
Project for Hotel at Pampulha, Minas Gerais.

Kubitschek House, Pampulha, Minas Gerais.

Theater, Belo Horizonte, Minas Gerais. Engineer: Joaquim Cardozo.

Project for Charles Ofair Residence, Rio de Janeiro.

Francisco Peixoto Residence, Cataguazes, Minas Gerais. Engineer: Albino Froufe.

Residence for Mrs. Prudente de Morais, Rio de Janeiro (originally planned for Pampulha) (1949). Engineer: Joaquim Cardozo.

1944
Nautical Club on the Lagoa Rodrigo de Freitas, Rio de Janeiro.

1945
Fluminense Yacht Club, Botafogo, Rio de Janeiro.

Project for Tribuna Popular Publishing Office, Rio de Janeiro.

Project for Hotel, Novo Friburgo, Rio de Janeiro.

1946

Boa Vista Bank, Main Office Building, Rio de Janeiro. Engineer: Joaquim Cardozo.

Boarding School, Cataguazes, Minas Gerais. Engineer: Albino Froufe.

1947

Centro Técnico da Aeronáutica (National Aeronautic Center and Housing Complex), São Jose dos Campos, São Paulo (1953).

Gustavo Capanema Residence, Rio de Janeiro.

Project for United Nations Headquarters, New York (with international design team headed by Wallace Harrison and Le Corbusier) (1952).

Burton Tremaine House, Santa Barbara, California.

1948

Project for a theater for the Ministry of Health and Education Building, Rio de Janeiro.

1949

Architect's Weekend House, Mendes, Rio de Janeiro.

Printing Offices for Empresas Gráficas o Cruzeiro, Rio de Janeiro (1950).

House for Mrs. Prudente de Morais, Rio de Janeiro.

Project for Monument to Rui Barbosa, Glória, Rio de Janeiro.

Project for Hotel Regente São Conrado, Rio de Janeiro.

1950

Duchen Factory, near São Paulo (with Helio Uchoa) (1953). Engineer: Joaquim Cardozo.

Project for Quitandinha Apartment-Hotel, Petrópolis, Rio de Janeiro.

Montreal Office Building, São Paulo.

Youth Club, Diamantina, Minas Gerais. Engineer: W. Muller.

1951

Copan Building, São Paulo (1957).

Tijuca Hotel, Diamantina, Minas Gerais (1952). Engineer: Joaquim Cardozo.

Conjunto Residencial Governador Kubitschek (Residential Complex "Juscelino Kubitschek"), Belo Horizonte, Minas Gerais (1958). Engineer: Joaquim Cardozo.

Julia Kubitschek Elementary School, Diamantina, Minas Gerais, (1952). Engineer: W. Muller.

Ibirapuera Park and Pavilions, São Paulo (with Helio Uchoa and Joaquim Cardozo) (1954).

Clube de Quinhentos, Guaratinguetá.

1952

Hospital Sul-América (today Hospital da Lagoa), Rio de Janeiro (with Helio Uchoa, Roberto Burle Marx, and Morales Ribeiro).

Service Station, São Paulo (1956).

Leonel Miranda Residence, Rio de Janeiro, begun 1954 (1955). Engineer: Joaquim Cardozo.

Project for Television Station for Diários Associados, Rio de Janeiro.

1953

Alternate Project for Quitandinha Apartment-Hotel, Petrópolis, Rio de Janeiro.

Office Building for Banco Mineiro da Produção. Engineer: W. Muller.

Canoas House, Rio de Janeiro (1954).

Middle School (Ginásio), Corumba, Mato Grosso do Sul, begun 1955 (1956). Engineer: J. Alvaris.

Middle School (Ginásio), Campo Grande, Mato Grosso do Sul, begun 1955 (1956). Engineer: José Garcia Neto.

Residence for B. Pigmatary, São Paulo. Engineer: Joaquim Cardozo.

Project for Ermiro de Lima Residence, Rio de Janeiro.

1954

Edmundo Cavanelas Residence, Petro do Rio, Rio de Janeiro (1955).

Project for Museu de Arte Moderna, Caracas, Venezuela.

Project for Airport Terminal Building, Diamantina, Minas Gerais. Engineer: W. Muller.

Middle School (Ginásio), Belo Horizonte, Minas Gerais, begun 1955 (1956). Engineer: Z. Glabe.

Project for TV Rio Television Station, Rio de Janeiro.

Apartment Building on the Praça da Liberdade, Belo Horizonte, Minas Gerais (1955).

State High School Auditorium, Belo Horizonte, Minas Gerais.

1955

Project for a Chapel for Brasília.

Project for Clube Libanês, Belo Horizonte, Minas Gerais.

Getúlio Vargas Foundation Headquarters, Rio de Janeiro (1958).

Intermark Headquarters, Niterói.

Apartment Complex for International Building Expo, Hansa Quarter, Berlin (1957).

Library, Belo Horizonte, Minas Gerais.

Eiffel Office Building, São Paulo.

1956

New City, Marina, Minas Gerais (with Nauro Esteves, Jose Reis, Lopes da Silva).

Temporary Residence, Catetinho, for President Juscelino Kubitschek, Brasília-Gama, Distrito Federal (today Museu Catetinho).

Alvorada Palace (Palace of the Dawn), Brasília (1958). Engineer: Joaquim Cardozo

1957

Brasília Palace Hotel, Brasília (1958).

Low-income Housing, 500 units, Brasília.

Banking Quarter, Brasília (first design altered).

Bus Terminal and Platform, Brasília.

Presidential Chapel adjoining Alvorada Palace, Brasília (1958).

1958

Project for a Library, Florianópolis, Santa Catarina.

Planalto Palace, Brasília (1960).

Federal Supreme Court, Brasília (1960).

National Congress Complex (1960).

Praça dos Tres Poderes (Plaza of the Three Powers), Brasília (1960).

Museum of the City of Brasília, Brasília (1960).

Rowhouses, Brasília (1960).

11 Ministry Buildings, Brasília (1960), with four ministries added by 1979.

Church of Nossa Senhora de Fátima, Brasília (1960).

National Theater, Brasília (1981). Engineer: Aldo Calvo.

1959

Residential Blocks for Superquadras, Brasília.

Metropolitan Cathedral, Brasília (1970), with glass panels by Marianne Peretti.

Residence for the President's Police, Brasília.

Hospital, Brasília (1962).

Sewage Purification Plant, Brasília.

1960

First Project, Palácio do Itamaraty (Ministry of Foreign Relations), Brasília.

Barracks, Military Sector, Brasília.

Palácio de Desenvolvimento (Institute for Metallurgy), Brasília.

Open-air Theater, Brasília (1962).

Brasília Tennis Club, Brasília.

Office Building "Barão de Mauá," Rio de Janeiro. Engineer: Sabino Barroso.

University, Main Building, Brasília (1962).

Project for Central Plaza, University, Brasília.

University-Ceplan Building, Brasília (1963).

Project for Dominican Cloister and Theological Institute, Brasília.

1961

Yacht Club, Brasília.

Project for Sports Center and Stadium, Brasília

1962

Headquarters and Exhibition Hall, Touring Club of Brazil, Brasília.

Ministry of Justice, Brasília (1970).

Palácio do Itamaraty (Ministry of Foreign Relations), Brasília, begun 1964 (1970). Engineers: Milton Ramos, Olavo Redig.

Annex to Yacht Club, Pampulha, Minas Gerais.

International Exposition Complex, Tripoli, Lebanon.

Mass Housing Complex, Brasília.

Project for Sports Center, Lebanon.

1963

Youth Sports Center (today Olympic Sports Center), Brasília.

Exhibition Composition, Grand Palais, Paris.

University of Haifa, Israel (with H. Muller, S. Rawett, and G. Dimanche) (1964).

Project for University, Ghana.

1964

Federmann Residence, Israel (with H. Muller, S. Rawett, and G. Dimanche).

Project for Ideal City of Neguev, Israel (with H. Muller, S Rawett, and G. Dimanche).

Congress Center and Business Quarter "Panorama," Tel Aviv, Israel (with H. Muller, S. Rawett, and G. Dimanche).

Nordia Residential Quarter, Tel Aviv, Israel (with I. Lothan, A. El Hanani, and D. Resnich).

Hotel Scandinavia, Tel Aviv, Israel.

1965

House for Edmond Rothschild, Israel.

Communist Party Headquarters, Paris (with J. de Roche, P. Chemetov, J. Prouve), begun 1967 (1971/1980).

Project for a Tourist Resort, Algarve, Portugal.

Project for Airport, Brasília.

Project for Government Palace, Brazzaville, Congo.

Project for Parliament Extension, "Palácio Vertical," Belo Horizonte, Minas Gerais.

Cesarea Building Complex, Israel.

Residence and School for Adolfo Bloch, Teresópolis, Rio de Janeiro.

1966

Manchete Publishing House, Rio de Janeiro (1981).

Park Hotel and Casino, Funchal, Madeira, Portugal (with Vianna de Lima) (1975).

Editorial Offices, Postille, Rio de Janeiro.

1967

Dominican Cloister, Sainte-Baume, France (1967).

Urbanization Project, Grasse, France (with Marc Emery).

1968

Temporary Building for Eucharistic Congress, Brasília.

University of Cuiabá, Mato Grosso.

Mondadori Publishing Building, Segrate, near Milan, Italy (with Luciano Pozzo) (1975).

Project for Satellite Station, Rio de Janeiro.

Ministry of the Army (including barracks), Brasília (1972).

Project for University, Algiers.

Project for a Mosque, Algiers.

Project for Civic Center, Algiers.

Hotel Nacional, Rio de Janeiro (1972).

Project for Music Center, Rio de Janeiro.

Residences in Cap Ferrat, France.

1969
University of Constantine, Algeria (1977).

Project for Barra 72 Exposition, Rio de Janeiro.

Headquarters and Hotel for Renault, Billancourt, near Paris (with P. Vigneront).

1970
Stadium, Brasília.

Institute for Brazilian Architecture, Brasília.

1972
Project for Business Center and Office Complex, Claughton Island, Miami.

Apartment Complexes, Barra de Tijuca, Rio de Janeiro (1982).

Maison de la Culture, Le Havre (1982).

Moura Lacerda University, Rio de Janeiro.

Urbanization Project, ZAC, Dieppe, France (with Marc Emery).

House for Frederico Gomes, Rio de Janeiro.

Bourse de Travail, Bobigny, near Paris (1980).

Denasa Office Building, Brasília.

Hotel Bahia, Salvador, Bahia.

Santo André Building Complex, São Paulo.

1973
Project for Student Dormitory, Oxford University.

Train and Bus Station, Brasília (1981).

Project, Tower for La Defense, near Paris.

1974
Project for Foreign Ministry Building, Algiers.

Project for Museum of the Earth, Sea, and Sky, Brasília.

House for Josephine Jordan, Rio de Janeiro (1978).

Telebras Office Building, Brasília (with Carlos Magalhães) (1978).

Residence of the Vice-President, Brasília.

Safra Bank, São Paulo (with gardens by Burle Marx).

1975
Foreign Ministry Annex, Brasília (1982).

FATA Office Building, Pianezza de Turin (with Riccardo Morandi, Massimo Gepmari), begun 1976 (1979).

Office Towers, Jidda, Saudi Arabia.

1976
Colégio Militar, Brasília (1979).

Headquarters of the National Party, Algiers.

Funerary Monument for Juscelino Kubitschek, Brasília.

Mirza House, Rio de Janeiro.

L'Humanité Headquarters, Saint Denis, near Paris (1980).

1977
Bus Terminal, Londrina, Paraná.

Project for Anthropology Museum, Belo Horizonte (with Darcy Ribeiro) (1978).

1978
Theater and Hotel, Vicenza, Italy (with Frederico Motterle).

Urbanization Project, Villejuif, near Paris (with Marc Emery).

Urbanization Project, Ilha Pura, Barra de Tijuca, Rio de Janeiro.

Urbanization Project, Curicica, Barra de Tijuca, Rio de Janeiro.

Manchete Publishing House, Brasília.

Ministry Annex, Brasília (1982).

Parliament Annex, Camara Annex IV, Brasília (1981).

Project for CESP Office Building (Compania Eléctrica de São Paulo), São Paulo.

Conference Center, Foz de Iguaçú, Paraná.

Institute for Nutrition, Constantine, Algeria.

Theater and Conference Center, Venice.

1979

Burgo Headquarters, San Mauro near Turin (with Frederico Motterle) (1984).

Praça Saens Pena Subway Station, Rio de Janeiro (with Glauco Campelle, Jose Luiz de Pinho, Sabino Barroso).

Project for a Zoo, Algiers.

Embratur Office Building, Brasília.

1980

Town Hall/Municipal Assembly, Vitória, Espírito Santo.

Project for Tiradentes Museum, Brasília.

Administrative Center for Pernambuco, Recife.

Library and Monument for Juscelino Kubitschek, Brasília (with Honorio Peçanha) (1981).

Project for Hotel and Convalescence Center (formerly Brasília Palace Hotel), Brasília.

Project for Monorail and Apartment Towers for Copacabana, Rio de Janeiro.

1981

Project for Convention Center for Libya.

Project for Hotel, Convention Center, and Apartment Complex (with Monument and Restaurant), Libya.

1982

Project for Monument for Carlos Fonseca Amador, Managua, Nicaragua.

Museum of the Indian, Brasília.

1983

Samba Stadium, Rio de Janeiro (1984). Structural Engineer: José Sussekind.

Centros Integrados de Educação Pública (CIEPs), State of Rio de Janeiro, begun 1984–86, many still under construction.

1985

Pantheon of Liberty and Democracy for Tancredo Neves, Brasília.

1986

Project for Monumento Tortura Nunca Mais, Rio de Janeiro.

1989

Monumento Volta Redonda (Memorial Nove de Novembro), Rio de Janeiro.

Memorial da América Latina, São Paulo. Structural Engineer: Jose Sussekind. (Parliament building completed 1992).

1991

Araras Theater, São Paulo.

Project for Memorial for Gorée Island, Senegal.

Museu de Arte Contemporânea, Niterói (under construction).

1992

Maison Brésil-Portugal, Lisbon (under construction).

1993

Project for Exposition Annex, Ibirapuera, São Paulo.

Project for Memorial to African Culture, Salvador, Bahia.

Notes

Introduction: Niemeyer and the Brazilian Dilemma

1. Roberto Damatta, *Carnivals, Rogues, and Heroes: An Interpretation of the Brazilian Dilemma*, trans. John Drury (Notre Dame, Ind.: University of Notre Dame Press, 1991), 3.

2. Allan Plattus, "Le Corbusier: A Dialectical Itinerary," in Deborah Gans, *The Le Corbusier Guide* (Princeton: Princeton Architectural Press, 1987), 9–25.

The Corbusian Discourse and the Architecture of Rio

1. The Ministry of Education and Health Building is discussed at length in the excellent analysis by Elizabeth Harris, *Le Corbusier: Riscos brasileiros* (São Paulo: Nobel, 1987). See also Yves Bruand, *Arquitetura contemporânea no Brasil* (São Paulo: Perspectiva, 1981), 81–93.

2. The winning project, submitted by Archimedes Memoria, was a monumental, stripped classical block in the style of Marcello Piacentini, but with a new twist: on the capitals of the entrance columns, Memoria used a subtle geometric ornament in the "Marajoara style," derived from the native Indians of the island of Marajó. The style was part of the revival of indigenous traditions that Memoria had sponsored while directing the Escola Nacional de Belas Artes. The ornament gives the project a vernacular Brazilian feeling that appealed to the traditional, nationalistic jury. The jury also favored Memoria's project because it was the only one among the finalists that followed budgetary guidelines.

3. Article 5 of Law 125, sanctioned on December 3, 1935, specified that "no large scale public building will be constructed without a previous competition for the selection of the project." Vargas responded to Capanema's request by promulgating Law 193, which stated in Article 1, paragraph 2: "The construction of the Ministry of Education and Public Health is not bound by the observance of the formality listed in Article 5 of Law no. 125 of December 3, 1935." See Harris, *Le Corbusier: Riscos brasileiros*, 65.

4. The content of Le Corbusier's important Rio semi-nars is discussed in Harris, *Le Corbusier: Riscos brasileiros*.

5. Lúcio Costa, personal communication with author, August 5, 1993.

6. Elizabeth Harris, interview with Carlos Leão, Rio de Janeiro, June 1981 (see Harris, *Le Corbusier: Riscos brasileiros*, 118).

7. "Projeto da construção do edifício-sede do MEC," vol. 6: "Planos" (Rio de Janeiro: Fundação Nacional Pró-Memória, n.d.). Niemeyer's drawings cannot be reproduced because the paper on which they were done has seriously deteriorated over the years. The ten-meter height of the pilotis also corresponded to the height of Celso Antonio's sculpture.

8. The drawing was published in Le Corbusier's *Oeuvre complete, 1934–1938* (Zurich: Les Editions d'Architecture, 1964), 81. See also Bruand, *Arquitetura contemporânea*, 85 n. 25.

9. Niemeyer, *A forma na arquitetura* (Rio de Janeiro: Avenir, 1978; my translation).

10. Niemeyer prompted Capanema to commission a work from Lipschitz to give the project an international flavor. Niemeyer's association with Bruno Giorgi would lead to a collaboration in the much more monumental context of Brasília.

11. Lúcio Costa, "Depoimento de um arquiteto carioca," *Correio da manhã* (Rio de Janeiro), June 15, 1951, reprinted in Alberto Xavier et al., *Arquitetura moderna brasilera: Depoimento de una geração* (São Paulo: Pini, 1987), 72–94 (my translation).

12. Goodwin was quoted in *A Noite* (Rio de Janeiro), July 2, 1942, 13. Goodwin and Kidder-Smith published the first modern evaluation of Brazilian architecture for the 1943 Museum of Modern Art exhibition "Brazil Builds: Architecture New and Old, 1652–1942." I am indebted to Kidder-Smith for allowing me to publish here several of his original photographs of the ministry, the Obra do Berço, the Lagoa House, and the Brazilian Pavilion.

13. Italo Campofiorito, "Brazilian Architecture up to the Present," *Arts and Artists* 11 (April 1976): 36.

14. Youssef Cohen, *The Manipulation of Consent: The State and Working-Class Consciousness in*

Brazil (Pittsburgh, Pa.: University of Pittsburgh Press, 1989).

15. See Gilberto Freyre, *Casa grande e senzala (The masters and the slaves)* (1930; reprint, Berkeley: University of California Press, 1986). Freyre argues that the colonial plantation house–slave shed assemblage represented an entire economic, social, and political system and was "a sincere and complete expression of the absorptive patriarchalism of colonial times" (xxxiii).

16. Le Corbusier, *Précisions* (Cambridge, Mass.: MIT Press, 1991), 13, 10, 9.

17. Le Corbusier, *Précisions*, 9.

18. Le Corbusier, "The Poem of the Right Angle," in Richard A. Moore, ed., *Le Corbusier: Myth and Meta-Architecture, The Late Period (1947–1965)*.

19. Niemeyer's oft-cited poem has been published on numerous occasions, most recently in Niemeyer, *Meu sósia e eu* (Rio de Janeiro: Revan, 1992), 58 (my translation).

Free-Form Modernism

1. Niemeyer was not the only modern architect to find a source of architectural forms in the female body. The work of the Puerto Rican art deco architect Pedro Mendez Mercado (1902–90) also explored this theme. See Enrique Vivoni-Farage, "Pedro Mendez Mercado: Workman of Puerto Rican Architecture," in *Pedro Mendez Mercado in His Time (1902–1990)* (exhibition catalog, Miami: Miami-Dade Community College, 1992).

2. The pavilion was published in *Arquitetura e Urbanismo* 3 (May–June 1939): 471–80. See also Stamo Papadaki, *The Work of Oscar Niemeyer* (New York: Reinhold, 1954), 12–17.

3. See *Arquitetura e Urbanismo* 2 (March–April 1938): 98–99.

4. Bruand, *Arquitetura contemporânea*, 105.

5. Bruand, *Arquitetura contemporânea*, 106.

6. Bruand, *Arquitetura contemporânea*, 134–36.

7. Bruand, *Arquitetura contemporânea*, 107–9.

8. Celino Borges Lemos, "A Pampulha como sonho de modernização," *Hoje em Dia* (Belo Horizonte), June 18, 1989, 6.

9. Kenneth Frampton, *Modern Architecture: A Critical History* (New York: Oxford University Press, 1980), 255.

10. Bruand, *Arquitetura contemporânea*, 112.

11. Niemeyer, *Oscar Niemeyer* (Lausanne: Alphabet, 1977), 217 (my translation).

12. Bruand, *Arquitetura contemporânea*, 114.

13. Niemeyer, *Meu sósia e eu*, 125 (my translation).

14. Bruand, *Arquitetura contemporânea*, 110, nn.119, 120.

15. Bruand, *Arquitetura contemporânea*, 106.

16. See Luciene Takahashi, *Minas Gerais*, October 28, 1988, 10–11; *Hoje em Dia*, July 6, 1989, 10–11.

17. Published in Willy Boesiger and Hans Girsberger, eds., *Le Corbusier 1910–1965* (Zurich: Artemis, 1960), 68–69.

18. See Bruand, *Arquitetura contemporânea*, 157.

19. Bruand, *Arquitetura contemporânea*, 153–55.

20. Quoted in Frampton, *Modern Architecture*, 257.

21. Niemeyer, "Oscar Niemeyer: Residência Canoas, Rio de Janeiro," *Módulo 70* (May 1982): 48 (my translation).

22. Quoted in H. Penteado, ed., *Oscar Niemeyer* (São Paulo: Almed, 1985), 72.

23. Ernesto Rogers, *Architectural Review*, October 1954, 239–40.

A Classicism for the *Sertão*

1. Niemeyer's major early writings are "Problemas atuais da arquitetura brasileira," *Módulo* 3 (December 1955): 19–22; "Depoimento," *Módulo* 9 (February 1958): 3–6; "A imaginação na arquitetura," *Módulo* 15 (October 1959): 6–13; "Forma e função na arquitetura," *Módulo* 21 (December 1960): 3–7. See also articles in *Módulo* listed in the selected bibliography. Niemeyer founded *Módulo* in 1955. The journal's title was inspired by the Modulor of Le Corbusier, whom Niemeyer invited to

220

serve on the editorial board.

2. See Niemeyer, *A forma na arquitetura*, 1978, 54 (my translation).

3. Niemeyer, "Depoimento," 3 (my translation).

4. Niemeyer, "Depoimento," 3–4.

5. Niemeyer, "Depoimento," 3 (my translation).

6. Papadaki, *The Work of Oscar Niemeyer*, 5.

7. Niemeyer, "Depoimento," 3 (my translation).

8. Niemeyer, "A catedral," *Módulo* 11 (1958): 1 (my translation).

9. Niemeyer, "Depoimento," 4 (my translation).

10. Niemeyer, "Depoimento," 4–5 (my translation).

11. The museum was published in "Museu de Arte Moderna em Caracas," *Módulo* 4 (March 1956): 37–45. See also Papadaki, *The Work of Oscar Niemeyer*, vol. 2, 82–99 (models, sections, plans, drawings).

12. F. Bullrich, *New Developments in Latin American Architecture* (New York: Braziller, 1969), 24.

13. Bruand, *Arquitetura contemporânea*, 182.

14. Niemeyer, "Museu de Arte Moderna em Caracas," 39–45 (my translation).

15. Niemeyer, "Problemas da arquitetura 7: Método de trabalho," *Módulo* 58 (April–May 1980): 86–89.

16. Norma Evenson, "Brasília: Yesterday's City of Tomorrow," in Wentworth Eldredge, ed. *World Capitals: Toward Guided Urbanization* (Garden City, N.Y.: Anchor Press, 1975), 476.

17. Cited in Evenson, "Brasília," 481.

18. See Norma Evenson, *Two Brazilian Capitals: Architecture and Urbanism in Rio de Janeiro and Brasília* (New Haven: Yale University Press, 1973); and more recently, James Holston, *The Modernist City: An Anthropological Critique of Brasília* (Chicago: University of Chicago Press, 1989).

19. See Lionello Puppi, *A arquitetura de Oscar Niemeyer* (Rio de Janeiro: Revan, 1987).

20. Niemeyer, "A Cidade contemporânea," *Módulo* 11 (1958): 5 (my translation).

21. Niemeyer, "A Cidade contemporânea," 5 (my translation).

22. As quoted in Lawrence Vale, *Architecture, Power, and National Identity* (New Haven: Yale University Press, 1992), 119 n. 44.

23. Vale, *Architecture, Power*, 125.

24. Niemeyer, "Unidade urbana," *Módulo* 12 (1959).

25. Cited in Vale, *Architecture, Power*, 125.

26. Niemeyer, "Depoimento," 6 (my translation).

27. Bruand, *Arquitetura contemporânea*, 190 n. 122.

28. Bruand, *Arquitetura contemporânea*, 200.

29. Bruand, *Arquitetura contemporânea*, 210.

30. Bruand, *Arquitetura contemporânea*, 210–12.

31. Niemeyer, personal communication with author, May 1990.

32. Niemeyer, *Oscar Niemeyer*, 149 (my translation).

33. Niemeyer, *Oscar Niemeyer*, 149 (my translation).

34. Niemeyer's thoughts on Brasília here and in the following paragraphs are from his prose poem "Nuvens" ("Clouds"), *Meu sósia e eu* (my translation).

35. Niemeyer, "Depoimento," 6 (my translation).

36. Bruand, *Arquitetura contemporânea*, 202.

37. Bruand, *Arquitetura contemporânea*, 206–7.

38. Niemeyer, as quoted in Gilbert Luigi, *Oscar Niemeyer: Une esthétique de la fluidité* (Marseilles: Parentheses, 1987), 22 (my translation).

39. Vale, *Architecture, Power*, 120 n. 46.

40. Vale, *Architecture, Power*, 120.

41. Vale, *Architecture, Power*, 126.

42. Vale, *Architecture, Power*, 126.

43. Evenson, "Brasília," 503.

44. Vale, *Architecture, Power*, 127; Holston, *The Modernist City*, 40.

45. See Niemeyer, "Pantheon Tancredo Neves," *L'Architecture d'Aujourd'hui* 251, June 1987, 4–5.

Niemeyer Abroad

1. Niemeyer, *Oscar Niemeyer*, 213.

2. H. Penteado, *Oscar Niemeyer*, 74.

3. William J. R. Curtis, *Modern Architecture Since 1900* (Englewood Cliffs, N.J.: Prentice Hall, 1987), 267–68. Curtis illustrates and discusses only Le Corbusier's Scheme No. 23A.

4. Niemeyer, *Oscar Niemeyer*, 215.

5. Niemeyer, *Oscar Niemeyer*, 214–15.

6. Niemeyer, *Oscar Niemeyer*, 215 (my translation).

7. See Victoria Newhouse, *Wallace K. Harrison, Architect* (New York: Rizzoli, 1989), chs. 11 and 12, esp. 125.

8. Max Abramovitz, interview with author, New York, March 23, 1991.

9. Niemeyer, *Oscar Niemeyer*, 225 (my translation).

10. Niemeyer, *Oscar Niemeyer*, 225.

11. Niemeyer, *Oscar Niemeyer*, 226.

12. Niemeyer, *Oscar Niemeyer*, 230–32.

13. Niemeyer, *Meu sósia e eu*, 54 (my translation).

14. Niemeyer, *Oscar Niemeyer*, 227.

15. Niemeyer, *Oscar Niemeyer*, 238 (my translation).

16. Niemeyer, *Oscar Niemeyer*, 239.

17. Niemeyer, *Oscar Niemeyer*, 240, 238 (my translation).

18. Niemeyer, *Oscar Niemeyer*, 285.

19. Niemeyer, *Oscar Niemeyer*, 286; Puppi, *A arquitetura*, 146.

20. Niemeyer, *Oscar Niemeyer*, 285.

21. Niemeyer, *Oscar Niemeyer*, 285; Puppi, *A arquitetura*, 120.

22. Christian Hornig, *Oscar Niemeyer: Bauten und Projekte* (Munich: Heinz Moos Verlag, 1981), 56–61.

23. Puppi, *A arquitetura*, 113.

24. Puppi, *A arquitetura*, 113; Niemeyer, *Oscar Niemeyer*, 273.

25. Luigi, *Oscar Niemeyer*, 35–36 (my translation).

26. Puppi, *A arquitetura*, 116.

27. Luigi, *Oscar Niemeyer*, 51, n. 14.

28. Niemeyer, *Oscar Niemeyer*, 295. His FATA headquarters in Turin (1976) used a similar structural solution in conjunction with an arcaded facade.

29. Puppi, *A arquitetura*, 116.

30. Niemeyer, *Oscar Niemeyer*, 297 (my translation).

31. Patrick Fils, "A une semaine de l'inauguration: Tout est prêt à l'Espace Oscar Niemeyer," *Havre Libre* (Le Havre), November 11, 1982, 3 (my translation).

32. Niemeyer, "O Centro Cultural do Havre," *Journal do Brasil* (Rio de Janeiro), December 11, 1982, 11 (my translation).

33. Patrick Fils, "L'Inauguration de l'Espace Niemeyer: 'Que tous et toutes y trouvent ce qu'ils cherchent,'" *Havre Libre*, November 19, 1982, 3 (my translation).

34. Fils, "A une semaine de l'inauguration," 3 (my translation).

35. Niemeyer, "O Centro Cultural do Havre," 11 (my translation).

36. Niemeyer, "O Centro Cultural do Havre," 11 (my translation).

37. As quoted in Niemeyer, "O Centro Cultural do Havre," 11 (my translation).

Late Works and Archi-Rituals

1. On Niemeyer's projects for the Barra de Tijuca, see "Oscar Niemeyer faz projeto para centro comercial da Barra," *Journal do Brasil*, December 4, 1969, 14.

2. Niemeyer, *Oscar Niemeyer*, 454.

3. Niemeyer, "Entrevista Oscar Niemeyer," *Módulo* 58 (April–May 1980): 26–27 (my translation).

4. See Darcy Ribeiro, *A universidade necessária* (Rio de Janeiro: Paz e Terra, 1978), and *Teoria do*

Brasil (Rio de Janeiro: Paz e Terra, 1972).

5. See "Niemeyer cria solução definitiva para o carnaval," *O Globo* (Rio de Janeiro), September 11, 1983, 23.

6. Jorge de Aquino Filho, "Oscar Niemeyer" (interview), *Fatos e Fotos/Gente* (Rio de Janeiro), December 19, 1983, 68–69 (my translation). See also, Governo do Estado do Rio de Janeiro, *A Passarela do Samba* (Rio de Janeiro: Avenir, 1983).

7. Governo do Estado do Rio de Janeiro, *A Passarela do Samba* (my translation).

8. Governo do Estado do Rio de Janeiro, *A Passarela do Samba* (my translation).

9. Sergio Augusto, "Niemeyer, a beleza ancorou na passarela," *Folha de São Paulo,* March 2, 1984, illustrated section.

10. Governo do Estado do Rio de Janeiro, *A Passarela do Samba.*

11. Alexandre Martins, "A volta de um velho destaque," *O Globo,* January 17, 1988.

12. See *Módulo* 91 (May–June–July 1984), special issue on the CIEPs.

13. "Nos Cieps abandonados, a educação cede vez a miséria," *O Globo,* March 6, 1990.

14. "Projeto: 500 bilhões de cruzeiros em escolas," *Afinal* (São Paulo), May 21, 1985, 42.

15. Simone Ruiz, "Os 'cemeterios' de Cieps," *Journal do Brasil,* June 19, 1991, 2.

16. "Nos Cieps abandonados."

17. "PDT projeta 5 mil Cieps para Collor," *Journal do Brasil,* May 14, 1991, 1.

18. Joan Dassin, ed.,*Torture in Brazil: A Shocking Report on the Pervasive Use of Torture by Brazilian Military Governments, 1964–1979, Secretly Prepared by the Archdiocese of São Paulo* (New York: Vintage Press, 1986), x.

19. See "Burle Marx condena projeto de Niemeyer," *Journal do Brasil,* November 5, 1986, and "Niemeyer responderá às críticas de Burle Marx," *Journal do Brasil,* November 6, 1986.

20. Eva Spitz, "Memorial Operário," *Journal do Brasil,* March 15, 1989, sec. B, 2 (my translation). See also the several articles in *O Globo* and *O Estado de São Paulo* for May 3, 1989, and the *Folha de São Paulo,* August 12 and 13, 1989.

21. Ribeiro's comments here and in the following paragraphs are from the special edition "Memorial da América Latina," *Módulo* 100 (March 1989): 11–13 (my translation).

22. Niemeyer's comments are from the special edition "Memorial da América Latina," 27, 37 (my translation).

23. Niemeyer, *Memorial da América Latina* (São Paulo: Fundação Memorial da América Latina, 1989), 12 (my translation).

24. Eduardo Galeano, *Open Veins of Latin America* (New York: Monthly Review Press, 1973).

25. Niemeyer, "Memorial da América Latina," 37 (my translation).

26. Niemeyer, "De Pampulha ao Memorial da América Latina," *Módulo* 100 (March 1989), 23 (my translation).

27. Niemeyer, "A Cidade contemporânea," 5 (my translation).

28. "Sogra pede teatro e Quércia atende," *O Estado de São Paulo,* January 27, 1991, 7 (my translation).

29. "Teatro da Sogra," *O Estado de São Paulo,* January 29, 1991 (my translation).

30. Paulo Buscato, "Quércia constroi teatro na terra da sogra," *O Estado de São Paulo,* January 27, 1991 (my translation).

31. De Aquino Filho, "Oscar Niemeyer" (interview), 68–69 (my translation).

32. Niemeyer, personal communication with author, May 1990.

33. See Sylvia Ficher and Marlene Milan Acayaba, *Arquitetura moderna brasileira* (São Paulo: Projeto, 1982), 7.

Selected Bibliography

General Works on Brazilian Architecture

Bruand, Yves. *Arquitetura contemporânea no Brasil.* São Paulo: Perspectiva, 1981.

Evenson, Norma. *Two Brazilian Capitals: Architecture and Urbanism in Rio de Janeiro and Brasília.* New Haven: Yale University Press, 1973.

Ficher, Sylvia, and Marlene Milan Acayaba. *Arquitetura moderna brasileira.* São Paulo: Projeto, 1982.

Fils, Alexander. *Brasília: Modern Architektur und Stadtplannung in Brasilien.* Dusseldorf: Beton Verlag, 1987.

Hitchcock, Henry-Russell. *Latin American Architecture Since 1945.* New York: Museum of Modern Art, 1955.

Holston, James. *The Modernist City: An Anthropological Critique of Brasília.* Chicago: University of Chicago Press, 1989.

Mindlin, Henrique. *Modern Architecture in Brazil.* New York: Reinhold, 1956.

Monographs on Niemeyer

Fils, Alexander. *Oscar Niemeyer.* Berlin: Frolich & Kaufmann, 1982.

Hornig, Christian. *Oscar Niemeyer: Bauten und Projekte.* Munich: Heinz Moos Verlag, 1981.

Luigi, Gilbert. *Oscar Niemeyer: Une esthétique de la fluidité.* Marseille: Parentheses, 1987.

Papadaki, Stamo. *The Work of Oscar Niemeyer.* New York: Reinhold, 1954.

———. *Oscar Niemeyer: Works in Progress.* New York: Reinhold, 1956.

———. *Oscar Niemeyer.* New York: Braziller, 1960.

Puppi, Lionello. *A arquitetura de Oscar Niemeyer.* Rio de Janeiro: Revan, 1987.

Spade, Rupert. *Oscar Niemeyer.* London: Thames and Hudson, 1971.

Articles by Niemeyer in *Módulo* (Rio de Janeiro)

"Problemas atuais da arquitetura brasileira." 3 (December 1955): 19–22.

"A capela de Ronchamp." 5 (1956): 40–45.

"Niemeyer fala sobre Brasília." 6 (1956): 8–23.

"Considerações sobre a arquitetura brasileira." 7 (1957): 5–10.

"Depoimento." 9 (February 1958): 3–6.

"A catedral." 11 (1958): 7–15.

"A imaginação na arquitetura." 15 (October 1959): 6–13.

"Forma e função na arquitetura." 21 (December 1960): 3–7.

"Joaquim Cardozo." 26 (1961): 4–7.

"Habitação pre-fabricada em Brasília." 27 (1962): 27–38.

"Consideracoes sobre a arquitetura." 44 (1976): 34–40.

"Viagens: Origens e influências na arquitetura." 46 (1977): 31–34.

"Problemas da arquitetura 1: O espaço arquitetural." 50 (1978): 54–61.

"Problemas da arquitetura 2: As fachadas de vidro." 51 (1978): 44–47.

"Problemas da arquitetura 3: Arquitetura e técnica estrutural." 52 (1978): 34–38.

"Problemas da arquitetura 4: O prefabricado e arquitetura." 53 (1979): 56–59.

"Problemas da arquitetura 5: O mercado de trabalho." 54 (1979): 94–95.

"Problemas da arquitetura 6: O problema estrutural e a arquitetura contemporânea." 57 (1980): 94–97.

"Entrevista Oscar Niemeyer." 58 (April–May, 1980): 26–27.

"Problemas da arquitetura 7: Metodo de trabalho." 58 (April–May, 1980): 86–89.

Special Editions of *Módulo* Dealing with Niemeyer

"Oscar Niemeyer." (1985).

"Brasília, 26 anos." 89/90 (1986).

91 (May–June–July 1984). On the CIEPs.

"Oscar Niemeyer, 50 anos de arquitetura." 97 (1988).

"Memorial da América Latina." 100 (March 1989).

Books by Niemeyer

Minha experiência em Brasília. Rio de Janeiro: Vitoria, 1961.

Quase memórias: Viagens, tempos de entusiasmo e revolta, 1961–1966. Rio de Janeiro: Civilização Brasileira, 1968.

Oscar Niemeyer. Milan: Mondadori, 1975 (French edition, Lausanne: Alphabet, 1977).

A forma na arquitetura. Rio de Janeiro: Avenir, 1978.

Rio: De provincia a metropole. Rio de Janeiro: Colorama, 1980.

Oscar Niemeyer. Ed. H. Penteado. São Paulo: Almed, 1985.

Meu sósia e eu. Rio de Janeiro: Revan, 1992.

Niemeyer par lui-même: L'architecte de Brasília parle a Edouard Bailby. Paris: Balland, 1993.